HIDDEN TRAPS
— OF THE —
INTERNET

HIDDEN TRAPS

— OF THE —

INTERNET

Building and Protecting Your Online Platform

JUDY L MOHR

Black Wolf Publications
PO Box 27008, Shirley
Christchurch 8640
New Zealand

blackwolfpublications.com

Copyright © 2024 by Judy L Mohr

Cover Design by Lesia T. (a.k.a. GermanCreative)
Interior Cover Design by River Dantzler

First Published 2024

ISBN-13: 978-1-7386251-0-9 (paper)
ISBN-13: 978-1-7386251-1-6 (ebook)

A catalog record for this book is available from the National Library of New Zealand.

To anyone who has ever felt overwhelmed by this beast known as the internet. Know that you are not alone.

Contents

1

INTRODUCTION
THE PLATFORM QUESTION

WHEN I FIRST STARTED on my own publication journey, I decided to learn everything that I could about what it would take to really get my writing out there. And there was this thing called a *platform* that kept cropping up.

Platform. Website. Platform. Social media. Branding. Platform. Platform.

And I started to freak out.

I had my first website back in 2000, and I remember quite clearly the headache that went into maintaining that thing. I didn't want to go down that road again if I could avoid it. But agents and publishers everywhere kept insisting that writers needed a platform and an active online presence.

Every time I turned around, there would be a mention of some new site that writers were expected to use. I wanted to break down into tears. This whole *building-a-following* thing was too much.

Then I learned the truth.

A writer's platform is not a website or social media. For that matter, it's not your books. A writer's platform is *everything* that you do to connect with your readers. It's about building connections with others—connections that could potentially help you throughout your career in various ways. A platform is the little things you do that will get you noticed.

A Writer's Platform

A writer's platform is made up of a lot of working parts that seem to fit together like a puzzle.

Yes, a writer's platform includes your books, website, and social media, and yes, this online component in today's market is important, but it's not everything.

It's your local writers' group that you attend once a month, or more frequently as the case may be. It's those conferences and book festivals you save your pennies for, so you can afford the registration. It's your participation in special events that have nothing to do with writing but might be vital for your research.

A writer's platform tells the world at large what issues are important to you and who you are as a writer. It highlights the things that interest you and what your readers might also be interested in. And it's the support network you have built around yourself to keep you motivated when times get hard.

A platform is *not* about marketing, promotion, or publicity. Sure, marketing activities can help to build a platform, but being vocal on social media saying *"Look at me!"* will not lead to a platform that gets you noticed in a good way. Those who spend all their time pushing that *"Buy my book"* message just annoy people. It's the fastest way to earn a bad reputation.

No, a platform is about forging those important connections, networking with both your readers and your colleagues. A platform is about building a community around you.

When you look at it in those terms, suddenly the idea of building a writer's platform is a little less scary. It's still hard, and it still takes a long time, but viewing a platform as a community-building exercise gives you permission to be yourself and experiment a little. You're reaching out to those who get you for being you.

The concept of a writer's platform is nothing new, though I will agree that the online component certainly has complicated things. But the most important thing to remember is that everything you do in building your platform is *uniquely you.*

No two platforms will be identical, because no two writers are identical. There might be similarities, but there will be significant differences too. And even better . . . a platform changes and grows as a writer changes and grows.

Nothing is cast in stone.

WHEN TO BUILD A PLATFORM

The best time to build a platform is now! Not tomorrow, or yesterday, but right now! Those connections that you forge as part of your platform are valuable in the extreme.

If you are new to writing, with no publications on the horizon, your platform will likely be about trying to connect with other writers and the publishing community as you learn your craft. Through your connections, you will find your critique partners, your beta readers, your mentors, and accountability buddies. But you will also discover that you're not alone, because you will meet other writers who are just as lost and confused as you are about this whole platform thing.

If you are getting ready to release your first book, your platform is likely getting ready to sprout wings as you start to dive into blog tours, advanced reader copies, and the review circuit. The connections you forge with others on the internet will help you keep your sanity as you navigate the chaos of dealing with Amazon, BookBud, Facebook Ads, and royalties.

For those who have been around the block a few times, you're going to be taking your preexisting platform and expanding it to incorporate new avenues and new ways to connect with readers. There is always a new technology that could be explored and new readers to reach out to.

At every step along the way, your platform should be a reflection of who you are as a writer and as a person. Never dive into any activities that aren't *you*. Only do the things you enjoy doing. Sure, give new ideas a go, but if they don't work and just aren't gelling with the way you want to do things, then don't force yourself to continue with something that will only make you look bad and stressed out.

SOME HARD TRUTHS

If you are reading this book, you've likely already made the decision to either start building a platform, redesign a preexisting one, expand your offline platform into the online world, or revive online components that have been left to collect cobwebs and dust. Regardless of the circumstances that have led you to this book, you are likely hoping that this book will make building the online aspects of a platform simple and easy.

Time for some hard truths.

1) Building a platform with a decent following is a lot of hard work.
2) There are no quick-and-easy solutions to this platform thing. You need to put in the time and effort.
3) And much of what you do will be trial and error, until you find something that works for you . . . only for the powers in control of the sites to change the algorithms, and you have to start all over again with your trial-and-error exercise. It's a constant experimental process because the algorithms are constantly changing.

Because building a platform is a lot of hard work with no quick-and-easy solutions, you need to have fun with it. If it feels like a chore, that attitude will show in your activities, and everything else you are doing will falter. Sure, there will be times when it feels like you're getting nowhere, shouting into the void, but nothing worth having was ever easy.

I have been building my personal writer's platform for over a decade now, and I still have a long way to go. This book contains just a fraction of the information that I've amassed along the way. I have made some mistakes—some *big* mistakes—and here is your opportunity to learn from those mistakes, so you don't have to make them yourself.

I can't tell you how to build the perfect platform to gain the best following. I can't tell you how to turn followers into book sales. And as much as I would love to, I can't tell you that all of this effort is worth it—because only you can make that decision.

But I can highlight some of the pitfalls and traps associated with online activities, showing you some of the tricks to mitigate the security risks. I can provide insights into the tools available to help make your online activities manageable. And I can show you how I have built my own platform, explaining why I've made certain choices.

While some of my comments will be reflective of offline activities, this book focuses primarily on the common online components of a writer's platform. The intention is to provide you with a road map that you can use to start planning your journey.

THIS BOOK

This book is *not* a book on how to market your books, turning your book into a best-seller, or how to actually get people to sign up for your newsletter. If I had that information, I would be rolling in the dough and laughing all the way to the bank. But sadly, all I can do is provide you with some insights on how to stay safe online—and how to have fun with what you do.

This book provides an overview of building an online platform in a safe manner. Because of how quickly internet technology changes (which is definitely faster than the publication cycle), emphasis is given to the concepts and ideas rather than site specific settings.

The information in this book has been divided into four main topics.

First up will be a discussion about internet security in general, looking at our common practices.

With the foundations in place about internet security, we'll then turn our attention to this thing called *branding* and look at how we can employ it across all of our activities—not just the online ones.

From there, we'll examine the common components of an online platform, including a website, the newsletter (or email list), and our social media activities. Then we will dive into some of the topics that writers of today need to think about, such as artificial intelligence.

At every step along the way, I'll be highlighting some of the hidden traps that might exist.

Just remember that there is no one-size-fits-all to this platform thing. Take on board only the suggestions that resonate with you.

PART ONE
INTERNET SECURITY 101

2
Types of Internet Security

It's common for writers to think of internet security as just the settings on a site or the login-and-password conundrum. Sure, these are part of it, but there are many components that work together to keep ourselves safe online.

Let's be real here. It isn't just our accounts that we're trying to keep safe. It's not just our physical persons. And it's not just our wallets.

It's also our mental health and our reputations.

Broadly speaking, internet security falls into three categories: site settings, our practices, and what we post.

Site Settings

Every online site we use will have its own settings to determine what is public, what is private, and what is in between. The site settings are typically a series of toggle switches or dropdown menus that we can take advantage of . . . or not.

But the sites are not static. Policies change and systems evolve. And the settings involved are constantly changing.

The settings revolving around who can send a private message on Facebook have changed multiple times over the years—and I joined the site in 2006.

Because of the fluid nature of site settings, we are not going to dive into the specifics of any given site in this book. That said, I highly recommend that you go through the settings on the various sites you use. Make sure that you understand what every setting does and that you are using it in the way that best suits you. Look for anything that is granting the public access to your information by default and make sure that you are happy to share that information. If not, change the settings!

And whenever you notice a change in the interface, check those settings again. The odds are something else has changed under the hood. Facebook is notorious for this. Twitter isn't much better. I mean, Twitter isn't even called Twitter anymore. (What sort of name is X anyway?)

OUR PRACTICES

When talking about the practices we employ, I'm referring to the way we manage logins, emails, passwords, computer maintenance, software management, etc. It's a big list.

We writers are often amongst the laziest people when it comes to security. We all know that we should be using different passwords for everything, but honestly, how many of us actually do that? Or how many people wouldn't know who they were if their internet browsers didn't save their login information for them? And how many of us use the same email for *everything*?

You will find a longer discussion on this security category in the next chapter, but before we get too carried away, we better define the third security category.

WHAT WE POST

The first two categories possess aspects that are at the mercy of some external factor, be that finances or the developers who created the site we're using. We are forced to make choices to mitigate the risks. However, this last category is 100% in our control. It is also the most dangerous to the average internet user.

This category encompasses the way we interact with others online. It's the images that we share and the things we say. It's our responses to messages and other posts. And it's the subtext that runs throughout everything we do.

For most of us, we might think nothing of the little joke we share with our followers. It's an innocent post that fits perfectly within our branding and platform. But that one post has the power to go viral and blow up in our face.

I hold no delusions of grandeur here, but one misinterpreted tweet can destroy your career in the blink of an eye. Don't believe me? Just look up what happened to Roseanne Barr. One tweet—which was supposedly sarcastic, but sarcasm in written form often requires something much longer than a tweet—and her brand-new TV show was canceled after airing only one episode. Nearly 40 years in the entertainment industry, and her career was trashed by one tweet.

You also have cyberstalking and cyberbullying. And if you think that the writing industry is immune to these things, boy, do I have some news for you.

Our private messages also fall into this category, because when it comes to the internet, nothing is private. One screen capture is all it takes.

Because of how dangerous what we post can be to our lives and our careers, we will be spending a significant amount of time on the last category in the later chapters of this book.

But before we go much deeper into the last category, let's take a closer look at our internet security practices.

3

GOOD INTERNET PRACTICES FOR WRITERS

IT STARTS WITH THE COMPUTER

FOR A WRITER, OR any freelancer, our computers are our most prized possessions. If that computer dies, we cry. And many of us are nursing machines that might be in need of defibrillation at any moment.

I'm not going to go into the advantages of Windows vs Mac. Seriously, peeps, this is a personal preference. (I personally prefer Windows.) But regardless of the operating system you use, all computers today have multiple security features built into the operating system. Use them!

It might be annoying, and you might be the only person who ever uses that machine, but add a username and password to log in, especially if you take your laptop (or mobile device) out of the house. The four-digit pins and fingerprint logins will work here, too.

Not to be the messenger of doom here, but what if someone steals your machine? Remember that those machines are connected to every facet of your life. Without the login requirement, you are effectively giving a thief the access codes to your accounts.

UPDATE YOUR OPERATING SYSTEM AND PROGRAMS

Keep your computers up to date with the latest versions of the operating system.

No, I'm not telling you to run out and get the latest version of Windows if you like the version that you're on. And Mac users will only be allowed to update their operating systems so far before the componentry won't take the new operating system. What I mean is to actually run the system updates instead of continually delaying them, ignoring them for months on end.

You can set these to auto-update, or you can run them manually. Even with the auto-updates turned on, there will be times when you have to go in and manually update a program.

Run updates on all the programs that you use regularly, not just your operating system. Keep your word-processing program of choice up to date. Update your web browser. Update your email editor.

Part of those updates often include security updates, fixing weak points where people have been hacked in the past.

If your programs are not set to auto-update, you can normally find a *Check for updates* option somewhere under the *Help* menu for the program. Sometimes, it's hiding on the *About program* popup dialog.

USE A VIRUS CHECKER AND FIREWALL

Most new computers come with a free license, typically for one year on whatever system the manufacturers have a partnership with. On Windows machines, it tends to be McAfee. Even if this is all you have, it's better than nothing.

And yes, I'm recommending that you have a paid virus checker on your computers, because the protection provided by the paid systems is that much better than the free ones.

The program your computer came with won't necessarily be the best on the market. Check out independent reviewer sites for information on the best virus checker and firewall programs, limiting your searches to articles posted in the last year.

The best independent review sites include:

• PC Magazine (pcmag.com),
• PC World (pcworld.com), and
• Macworld (macworld.com).

There are others, of course, but for the platform specific stuff, these sites would be my first port of call. They have been around for years (and I mean years . . . at least a decade for all sites), and none of them are financially tied to Microsoft or Apple.

But let's jump ahead, assuming that you are using a machine in good working order, with an up-to-date operating system and the latest version of your favorite software, and that you are running a good virus checker and firewall program.

BROWSER MAINTENANCE

The next danger point is our internet browser. I'm not going to dive into the benefits of Safari, Chrome, Firefox, Edge, or whatever other browsers are out there now. But I do need to remind you that all browsers collect *cookies*.

Cookies are packets of data that whiz around the internet, going between a website and your computer, communicating information about logins, visit statistics, and other wonderful things. They do many neat things, including remembering who you are in case you have a minor brain fart and forget yourself. It's the cookies in your browser that tell Facebook that you have already logged into the site. And it's the cookies that tell those pesky popup windows to leave you alone for a while.

Whenever you visit a site, one of the first things that it does is ask your computer for the cookies stored on your system. It's like a little handshake between your internet browser and the remote server. If the wrong funky handshake is used, then you'll get asked to log in again.

If you don't want the delicious home-backed scripts, you can block them through your browser, but don't come crying to me when nothing works and you can't see anything on the internet.

However, too many cookies stored on your system can slow your internet speed down . . . and some cookies leave you open to security risks.

It is recommended that you *clear your browser cookies on a regular basis.* You can find these tools in your browser settings.

I recommend that you clear your cookies once a month at a minimum, but I know others who clear them daily. In fact, there is a setting on your browsers that will clear cookies every time you close the browser program down. The only downside of this is that every time you clear your cookies, you have to log into your accounts again. That can get a little tiresome.

When I clear my cookies, I also clear my browser history. No point in remembering where I've been when I'm more focused on where I'm going.

Occasionally, I'll also clear the stored passwords, but this leads me into the next security issue with our practices.

Password Security

How many of you rely on the passwords saved on your favorite browser to remember who you are? And how many of you have your devices linked, so those passwords migrate from device to device using the same browser program?

And if you are using the same password for everything . . .

Look, I get it. Keeping track of passwords can drive anyone to the brink of madness, especially if you have the number of accounts that I do. Sometimes, simplicity wins out. Hell, even I have my browser remember the passwords for certain accounts, because I too am that lazy. But even I won't use the same password for everything. That's just asking for trouble.

For those interested in using a third-party password management app, run a Google search (or whatever search engine you want to use), and look at the review sites. PC Magazine, PC World, and Macworld are going to be your friends by the time we're done.

If you choose to go with the simplicity of using the browser to remember who you are, there are certain passwords that should never be saved to your browser. I'm talking about the login passwords for your bank, PayPal, government sites (like taxes), and other vital systems that would be devastating if they were ever hacked.

Use strong passwords: a mixture of upper and lower case, numbers and letters, and symbols.

TWO-FACTOR AUTHENTICATION

For every system possible, especially accounts connected to money, use what is known as two-factor authentication (2FA).

2FA comes in a variety of forms, ranging from sending you text messages with codes, emails with codes (or special login links), or codes generated by authenticator apps on your phone. But the essence of how the various 2FA systems work is all the same. You log in to the site and you'll be asked to take an additional login step to prove you have authority to access that account.

There was a time when I didn't use 2FA. In fact, when I released my original internet security book back in 2017, I proudly pointed out that I wasn't that paranoid about hackers on social media sites. But today, it's not just social media that uses the internet.

Every facet of my life—banking, taxes, my medical records—no exception—is floating around on the internet. It's no longer about protecting the nude baby photos of my son. It's now about protecting my house, my livelihood, and my identity.

Not every system will call it 2FA. My bank calls it *OnlineCode.* I suppose that is an accurate description of what the feature is for. But whatever it's called, USE IT!

It's surprising the number of hackers that could have been stopped in their tracks if people would just use 2FA.

And where possible, turn on the notifications that tell you when someone has logged in to your accounts. Yeah, those notifications can be annoying if you log in and log out of your account a lot, but if you get that notification and you know that you didn't log in to your account . . .

Hello, hacker, whatever it is you're trying to do is not going to work—not today.

> WARNING (and you'll get a few of these throughout this book): When setting up 2FA on your accounts, try to set up multiple methods. Don't rely on just your authenticator app. *Always* download backup codes if you are given the option. If you lose access to your phone, that backup code will be your lifesaver.

Trust me on this. I've been there—done that—and I got burned.

AUTHENTICATOR AND PASSWORD APPS

Authenticator apps are special apps that you load onto your mobile device that will generate new unique six-digit codes every minute. When setting up an authenticator app 2FA protocol for a particular site, you will often be given a QR code to scan within your chosen authenticator app. (A QR code is a funky two-dimensional barcode that mobile devices seem to magically understand.) With the QR code scanned, you'll be given your first six-digit code, which you enter back into the site you're logging into. This completes the connection.

Authenticator apps are a handy, in-your-pocket way of proving that you have authority to access that account.

However, I should highlight that not all authenticator apps are the same when it comes to security.

Google Authenticator is one of the most common systems referred to. However, at the time of writing this book, the Google Authenticator app did not employ any additional security protocols other than those used to sign in to your phone. So, if you could get into the phone, then you are in the Google Authenticator app.

The same is true with the Google Wallet app (previously known as Google Pay).

This makes me nervous in the extreme, because anything loaded into Google Wallet or Google Authenticator is only as safe as the password or security measures used to get into my phone.

Have you seen Netflix's series of *You*? All Joe had to do to get into the phone of the dead person in front of him was hold the phone to the person's face. And Joe had access to everything from there. Why is it that fiction can see where things can go horribly wrong, but we still have a habit of ignoring the danger?

I stopped using Google Authenticator a long time ago, moving to an authenticator app that used additional biometrics to open the app. Microsoft Authenticator is one such app. Is it the best on the market? Definitely not, but it's more secure than the Google equivalent.

Password management apps are different beasts again. These are apps used to store your login information (username and passwords) behind some sort of security firewall. All phones come with a built-in password management system, but you can also get apps that you can use within your computer browsers. Whatever digital system you choose, ensure that your data is safely hidden behind multiple layers of protection.

And for those thinking about recording all of their passwords the old-fashioned way, using a pen and a notebook, I'm not going to stop you. Just made sure that your notebook of passwords is safely stored where you can access critical information in the event of a fire or natural disaster. Hate to say it, but floods and cyclones have a bad habit of destroying anything recorded on paper.

To get an idea of the best authenticator apps and password management systems on the market, check the reviews on sites like PC Magazine, PC World, and Macworld. (Yep, it's those sites again. There is a reason I keep pointing you to them.)

SPECIAL NOTE ON GOOGLE 2FA

Google seems to be one of those systems that easily gets upset if you decide to do something outside of normal operations. This includes upgrading your phone or running a factory reset.

The moment you either upgrade your phone or run a factory reset, you lose access to your authenticator app. It's the one system that is not backed up to Samsung accounts or iCloud, or whatever system that you are using to back up your phone and app data. This is a deliberate security feature designed into iPhones and Android devices.

BUT if you haven't taken the time to set up multiple 2FA methods on a Google account, this may mean that you are locked out of portions of your account. A recovery email or recovery phone may give you access to your email or your Google Drive, but you won't be able to change anything on the management side of the account. You'll be able to see the settings, but you won't be able to change them . . . not without access to the particular 2FA method for your account.

So, you can get your data (the bit that you were trying to protect by using 2FA), but you won't be able to secure your account again.

How do I know this? Well . . . Back in 2022, I ran a factory reset on my phone. I thought I had backup codes for all of my Google accounts. I was wrong. As a result of the phone reset, I lost access to the security side of three critical accounts. DOH! I was forced to move all external accounts that were connected to the affected Google accounts to another email and delete (or abandon) the now-insecure accounts.

Trust me, this is one mistake you don't want to make. It's a mess to fix, especially if you don't keep detailed records about what accounts are connected to what emails.

With Google accounts (and any other account), ensure that you have multiple 2FA methods. Setting up a recovery phone is not enough. You need to actually enable the phone to be used for the 2FA process. I would also ensure that you have downloaded (and saved in a safe location) a list of backup codes.

IT'S BASIC STUFF . . . UNTIL IT'S NOT

Everything that we have talked about so far are basic practices. Some of us will have been doing these things in our sleep, while others will have been avoiding them out of fear (or possibly just laziness), but that's just the beginning.

There are more concepts to incorporate into our security practices that will help to build extra layers of security in our online activities.

4
EMAILS FOR WRITERS

EVERYTHING WE DO IN today's society tends to be connected to an email address. You sign up for a gym membership and they ask for your email. Newsletters from your children's school are sent home via email. My power bill and bank statements are also sent by email.

As writers, this quickly becomes complicated by all the newsletters and blogs we subscribe to and the communications have with beta readers and editors. Add submissions for publications into the mix, and you have a muddled mess.

In building an active online presence, a single email address is not enough. At a minimum, you will want six (6) email addresses just for your writer-related activities, ideally eight (8) or more. Yes, six to eight emails. This might seem like overkill, but before you discount the idea, let me break it down for you.

EMAIL 1: ADMINISTRATION

The first email you'll need will be your *account administration email*. This email will be the one that you use to sign up for the things connected to money. When those royalty checks come in, or if there are bills to be paid, this is the email that will be notified.

Do not use this email for general communication. Keep it as secret as possible. If someone were to hack into your system, this would be the email that they are really after.

Security of your accounts instantly improves if people don't know this email exists.

You might also use this email for the registration of your domains—that is, of course, assuming that you have elected to purchase privacy protection on your domains, which is a little feature from your domain provider that hides your contact details in a WHOIS (pronounced "who is") search. (We'll talk more about WHOIS searches in *Chapter 17: Self-Hosting: Should I?*)

Remember that you want to keep this email as secret as possible. If you aren't using privacy protection, either by choice or because the option isn't available to you (some domain extensions don't allow privacy protection on them), then you will want to use a *secondary administration email* for your domain registration.

> WARNING: Avoid using an email from your internet provider as your administration email.

For a moment, let's consider the situation where you moved to a new residence. You might be forced to change internet providers and potentially be locked out of your systems. If you had used that now-disconnected email to register a domain, you would encounter major problems in transferring domains to different hosting providers. Domain transfers need to be conducted through the email you originally registered the domain under.

> WARNING: Under no circumstances should you use an email from a custom domain as your administration email.

Should something happen to that domain—you change it or it gets canceled for some other reason—you will encounter the same problem as you would if you were forced to change internet providers.

> **WARNING:** Do not have your domain registration connected to a domain email address. If you lose access to the domain email, then you lose control over your domain.

Yeah, I know that I'm repeating myself, but please, I beg you, for the sake of your internet security, don't try to be *smart* on this one. Stick with the simple solutions.

I recommend that your administration email(s) be a Gmail account. Yes, Gmail has its own issues, but you can have as many of those things as you want for free, so at least the extra accounts aren't costing you money.

EMAIL 2: SECONDARY ADMINISTRATION

There are instances where registration for certain things becomes a matter of public record. But it is still important that you maintain separation of accounts for sanity and security. To help with this, you will want to have a *secondary administration email*.

For those who are self-publishing, you might want to use this email for the Amazon account that you use for the sale of your books. I would also be inclined to use this email during the purchase of your ISBNs and registering your copyright.

For those who are traditionally publishing, you might use this email for your Amazon Author Central or Amazon Affiliates account.

If you have elected to forgo with privacy protection on your domain registration (a stupid idea in my opinion), or if you have a domain extension where privacy protection isn't an option, then you will want to use your secondary administration email for your domain registration.

This is because without privacy protection on your domains, your email address becomes a matter of public record. And you don't want the email connected to your bank and taxes to be publicly known. That's a disaster waiting to happen.

EMAIL 3: SOCIAL MEDIA ADMINISTRATION

This will be the email that you will use to sign up to sites such as Facebook, X (formerly known as Twitter), Mastodon, Instagram, or any other social media account.

Social media accounts are highly susceptible to hacking. The number of times we hear about another breach on yet another social media site is insane. But with each site hacked, the connected email address becomes compromised.

By isolating your social media accounts from the rest of your platform, you create a barrier that protects your money, your website, and your author accounts.

If a simple practice of using a different email for your social media will protect your finances and your books, why wouldn't you do it?

MY ADMINISTRATION CRAZY

I, myself, actually have four administration emails:

- personal activities—connected to my household utilities, my taxes, and my bank;
- front-end business accounts—which includes my web-hosting and email list management;
- backend business accounts—including PayPal and other similar accounts; and
- a fourth connected to publisher accounts.

On top of this, I also have three social media administration emails, one for each persona that I have online: the writer, the editor, and the publisher.

All of my administration accounts are Gmail accounts. That way I can leave my custom domain emails for communications with others.

A writing buddy of mine decided that she wanted to give each of her publishing accounts its own administration email. I think she was up to eight administration emails for just her indie-publishing accounts when I last spoke to her.

It can be confusing, but by having this division of administration, you separate the different aspects of your personal platform into their different components, isolating the risks. It also gives you the ability to easily bring on an assistant to help with tasks like web administration, newsletters, or, for that matter, social media. Not all accounts provide the facility to add multiple logins, and you don't ever want to give a stranger access to anything that is connected to money.

EMAIL 4: GENERAL COMMUNICATIONS

The next email in this list is the email that you've added to your business cards. It's the email that you give out to people you meet. Its purpose is general communications.

No bills are going here (unless you are desperate to have the bills go to your general communications email). However, you know that any email going here is something that will need your attention at some point.

Aunt Sally will be wanting a copy of that chocolate cake recipe, and she might pester you until you send it.

I would be inclined to use this email for contact with your critique partners, beta readers, and ARC readers.

This email will normally be some variant of your pen name. It's entirely up to you whether this is an internet provider email, a custom domain email, or a Gmail. Just be smart about the name connected to this email.

As much as we hate to admit it, people do judge others based on first impressions. Make sure that your first impression through email is the best it can be.

If you're like me, you'll have a communications email for personal communications (the email I give to family, friends, and my children's schools when they were still in school), and another for your communications with your writing friends. If you are operating a business too, ensure that you have an additional email that is for business communications.

EMAIL 5: PUBLIC-FACING COMMUNICATIONS (OPTIONAL)

Because of the way the internet works, any email listed on a website will be scraped by bots and will eventually become the target of scammers. Accept it now. But to help with the scammer insanity, you can use a *public-facing communications email* that is separate from your general communications email.

If you were to use a *public-facing communications email*, this email would be listed on your website and anywhere else where some random internet user will be able to find your email address.

If you have an email mailing list (and I hope you do), this would also be the email that your newsletters are coming from.

But when you respond to any email that goes to this public-facing communications email, you can shift it to your general communications email.

A little Black Wolf secret: While the public-facing communications email for my editorial business is real, the public-facing communications email for my writer persona is not. However, in both cases, any emails sent to the public-facing emails are forwarded to the general communications emails for their respective domains. I have done this so I can easily set up assistant accounts should the need ever arise.

EMAIL 6: SPAM

The next email on this list is the *spam email*. This email is intended for use on those *"Send me something for free"* websites, where you know they'll just send you spam. If it goes to an email intended for that purpose, who cares?

Yeah, I know, I'm messing around with the subscriber statistics here, but I have a strategy for that too. Just hold on.

Use your spam email for those frequent shopper cards, too. Let's face it, those emails are nothing but spam.

For the sake of your sanity, I would recommend that you obtain this email address from a service like Gmail.

As I write this book, all free Google accounts have access to 15 GB (gigabytes) of disk space. That's a lot of email. So, if you only log into the account say every three months, just to clean it out, then who cares? You can also set up filters that will automatically delete any messages over a certain age. With filters like that in place, you only need to log in when you actually want something that is being sent to that email.

EMAIL 7: SUBSCRIPTIONS (SPAM YOU WANT)

There is a special category of spam that is actually spam you want (which I suppose means that it's not really spam). I'm talking about the blog and newsletter subscriptions.

So, for those of you who were worried about messing around with the open rates on email lists, worry not. It's spam you want, so you're reading that stuff . . . most of the time.

However, if you're like me, you subscribe to an insane number of blogs and newsletters. If I'm away for the week and don't check my subscription email, I can easily come back to hundreds of emails waiting for me—all of which are actually spam, but it's spam I want.

By using a specially dedicated email for my newsletter subscriptions, I know that when the inbox is overloaded—because I haven't cleaned it out for a few days—I can do a generic *delete message*.

SPECIAL ADVICE: Connect WordPress.com accounts to your subscription email, not your administration email. This is because of the way WordPress.com works with blog subscriptions.

SPECIAL WARNING: Those with custom domains on WordPress.com websites, your bills will go to this account, but that's only once a year, and you can keep an eye out for them. Because of this, make this email a Gmail account or similar. You don't want to get locked out of your domain for any reason.

EMAIL 8: EDITORIAL/SUBMISSIONS (OPTIONAL)

The last email on this list is an email address dedicated to communications with editors, agents, or other industry service providers.

With the amount of standard communications that can occur, any important emails from parties that you send your manuscripts to could easily be missed. By having a dedicated email for this special type of communication, you can set alarms and alerts that bring those emails to your immediate attention.

You might want to use this email for your critique partners and beta readers, but that one is entirely up to you. I use my general communications email for discussions with critique partners and beta readers, leaving this email for the critical editorial reports and publisher contracts.

With a submissions email, I recommend using some variant of the name you write under. Some might be tempted to create a *submissions@domain.com*, but this format of email address is commonly used as the address that people send submissions to.

A Lot of Emails

I will be the first to admit that the number of emails mentioned above seems crazy and complicated, but trust me, it makes things simpler. Each email has its dedicated purpose, so you know exactly what type of email communications are expected to be in those accounts.

In practice, you can use as many emails as you feel is necessary. You don't need to check every email all the time. I keep a close eye on my communications emails, but log into the others about once a week to see if there are any administrative matters that I need to attend to. If I'm expecting something in particular, I'll keep a closer eye on them.

And my spam email is something that I log into perhaps once every three months. I take a quick skim to see if there was anything that I was actually interested in (like that $25 gift card to my favorite stationery store that was sent for my birthday), then I just delete all the messages and move on.

Document what accounts you have connected to what email. This will help you in the event that an email ever becomes compromised or you lose access to it.

To help you get started with your email setup, I've created a checklist with little reminders of the things that you need to be on the lookout for along the way.

You can access the checklist and all other supplementary materials for this book at:

blackwolfeditorial.com/hidden-traps-book

Transitioning to New Emails

For the moment, I'm going to assume that you have been using one email for multiple types of activity and would like some insights on how to make those transitions go smoothly.

Step One: Breathe.
Step Two: Document what accounts (and activities) are
connected to what emails as you go.
Step Three: Make the transition in stages.

If you are changing the login emails, then go into the affected accounts and make those changes. No further action should be required (except documenting the change for your records).

To change the email for your blog and newsletter subscriptions, the way that email is changed will depend on the email list management systems used by the external party. In some systems, you have a "manage your subscription" link—typically found at the bottom of the emails—where you can just change the email yourself. For some systems, you'll need to unsubscribe so the old email is removed from the database, then resubscribe using the new email. And for other systems . . . Well . . . Some people aren't using legally compliant systems (and I shall roll my eyes at this idiocy now), and you might need to get them to change the email in the database for you.

Be prepare for this type of transition to take a few months. If you're like me, you have no idea which blogs and newsletters you subscribe to until they come in.

If you are moving general communications to another account, make people aware of the change of email address (no explanation is required), and reply to the incoming emails from the new account. There will be the odd person who insists on using the old email address, but if you keep replying from the new address, eventually they'll get the hint and use the new one.

GMAIL AND INTERNATIONAL TRAVEL

Be warned that Gmail (and a Google account, in general) is locked to the country you were in when you signed up for the account.

For most of us, this won't be an issue, because most of us aren't jetsetters, constantly traveling around the world. But for the small number of us who are constantly on the move, this can limit your access to certain Google features as you travel.

Yes, you can change the country that your account is "registered" to, but if you make that change, then you won't be able to change it back for one year. And when you change your country, you won't be able to access your Google Play balance . . . or some of the apps . . . or books, or whatever.

This can also impact Android devices and Chrome browsers.

Because of this little Google quirk, if you travel a lot, then you might want to set up separate Google accounts for the different countries that you visit, just so you can access the Google features.

Otherwise, don't stress about it and keep moving forward.

(It was my writing buddy who frequently travels between Australia, Canada, United Kingdom, and New Zealand that highlighted to me this particular hidden trap.)

5

FOILED BY THE BAD PRACTICES OF OTHERS

ALL THE HARD WORK that we put into building the best practices could easily be foiled by the bad practices of others. Your carefully selected emails and account information could be compromised by the things that others do.

Here is an example.

When sending an email to a group of people, it is best practice to send that email using the blind carbon copy, or BCC, as it is often listed in email editors. In fact, an even better idea is to use an email management system that keeps everyone's emails private, and people get to choose if they want those emails or not. But regardless of how you send your group emails, unless the recipient has given you permission to share your email address with others, you are breaking the law if you choose to ignore best practices for email communications and use CC (carbon copy) or the TO address lines for that group.

There are exceptions to this law-breaking behavior, of course, which includes internal emails sent as a company-wide announcement to company domain emails.

However, some people don't care and will knowingly break the law, or they don't know the proper way to do things. The end result is the same: your email address is made public by someone who isn't you . . . and without your permission for that information to be shared with the world at large.

When I was studying for my diploma in business management during 2022, I deliberated about signing up for the course under my business email or my administration email. When I got the first email from the course coordinator, I was grateful that I chose to use my public business email address. That first email was sent to everyone on the course with everyone's email address listed in the TO field. As a result, everyone enrolled for the course had my email address . . . and I had theirs.

When I highlighted to the course coordinator that what he had done was actually illegal (and I wasn't the only person to bring this to his attention), he told me he *didn't care.* He thought it was best that we all had each other's emails, so we students could communicate amongst ourselves.

While his intention had merit, he never asked for permission to share our email addresses with the class. There were others on the course who had used private emails and were peeved, because they would have preferred that their business emails be shared, not their administration emails. But the course coordinator never gave us a choice. *He didn't care.*

It was minor justice to know that his own email and domain got flagged as spam later that same year. He decided to send out a mass marketing email to all those who had done the course in the past, and Google didn't like that. I laughed my head off when I saw the email *flagged as spam.*

When I gave my presentation a month later on my course project (which incorporated email list management), I made a point in saying that if you are going to send out mass emails, you should be using an email list management tool. "Saying that you can't afford it is not an excuse." At the time this book was published, MailerLite offered free accounts for up to 1000 subscribers.

But the example of my course coordinator sharing email addresses without permission is not the worst example I have.

In July 2023, a writing buddy of mine received an email from Spotify in relation to her Findaway account. Somewhere along the line, someone at Spotify decided it was a good idea to send the email directly to everyone with a Findaway account, including *all* email addresses in the TO field of the email. So, everyone got everyone's email address. And her email blew up, as everyone decided that it was a good idea to use the reply-to-all option, and in some cases, sending private financial information. Talk about a mess.

Spotify claimed that the offending email was a result of a system hack, which highlights a different issue, one that is even worse than a stupid email mistake. Regardless of whether it was a hack or not, the end result was the same: the emails connected to those accounts were compromised.

And one smarmy person decided that it was the perfect opportunity to advertise his book, sending his purchase links to everyone who was caught by the security breach. I shall roll my eyes and shake my head now. What a way to tank your reputation.

Facebook has seen breach after breach. Customer databases from service providers have been leaked. And the list goes on.

My point is that you can take every precaution you can, but when it comes to the internet, sometimes, you're at the mercy of the practices of others.

6

THE DANGERS OF WHAT WE POST

YOU TAKE A PHOTO of your latest adventure, and you want to share it with the world. You're excited. Rightly so. In your excitement, you upload that photo on Instagram, load the message with appropriate hashtags, add your location, and hit post. Your message (and photo) is whizzing around the world in cyberspace. Instant likes and shares, and your post is well and truly out there.

What you don't know is that you're being watched. Every detail of your life is being recorded.

Your feed might seem innocent enough. There are frequent posts about your morning coffee in that Starbucks cup, often followed by some image from the office. There's the lunch with the girls, and dinner with your parents to celebrate mom's birthday.

Creepy Bad Guy has been watching you for some time and has envisioned many a date with you—not that he's ever interacted with you. He's just watching your feeds. But he knows your daily routine and every other little detail that you had decided to share with the world.

But it's your latest photo that has inflamed Bad Guy. It's a photo from the baseball game with Random Date. Random Date is even tagged in the photo and mentioned in the caption by his handle. So, Bad Guy clicks on the link for Random Date's profile.

There, right at the top, is a photo of Random's truck, just after its latest spit-shine. And there in the photo is the license plate number. Motor vehicle registration records are publicly accessible. Just a bit of cash, and Bad Guy now has Random Date's address.

And Bad Guy has just progressed to the next level. He's a full-fledged stalker.

Some version of the above scenario *is happening right now* to countless men and women on social media. What's worse, they have no idea that it's happening. In many cases, it will never progress past voyeurism, but there will be the odd unsuspecting victim who *will* discover the real dangers associated with oversharing on social media. And it could cost them their lives.

And the reality . . . Random Date and Starbucks Coffee Chick have brought it on themselves. They let it happen.

It wasn't the site settings or account practices that created the problem. It was what they posted.

Coffee Chick needs to *stop* posting about her morning coffee with clues as to where she goes and when. She needs to stop posting things that reveal to the world her daily routines.

And Random Date needs to sanitize his account ASAP, removing all photos of his truck with his license plate showing. Remove any images with the letter box showing in front of his house. Remove anything that could give Creepy Bad Guy fuel for their stalker obsession.

And I wasn't lying when I said that motor vehicle registration records are publicly accessible.

In doing a little research, I discovered that even I can place a few phone calls to the vehicle registration authority in New Zealand and get an address for the person whom a particular vehicle is registered to. All it takes is time and a little cash—and I mean *little* cash, as in approximately $30. Though, in New Zealand, you can opt-out of the public registration database. (You can *opt-out!* Like we had a choice to opt-in in the first place. I shall roll my eyes now.)

That said, it would appear that Australia has got this particular little detail right—protecting everyone. While you can get a vehicle's motor history, you can not get the registered owner's private details. That doesn't mean that with a little smarts you can't get the information via other means.

But let's move away from Random Date and Coffee Chick. Now that Bad Guy has them in their sights, they're screwed anyway. For the moment, I want to shift this conversation to something that is a little closer to home.

PAST PHOTOS PUT US AT RISK

A few years ago, I ran a session on internet security for one of my writers' groups. In preparation for that session, I reached out to one of my creepy contacts and had them do me a favor. I had them go through the personal profiles of particular people—namely the other writers in the group—and dig up whatever details that they could by way of what was publicly available only. I knew they had access to more sinister means to get private details, but I just wanted to show the writers in the group the dangers associated with what they were posting. I wanted to scare them.

For the most part, the posts were innocent. From the post of one person, my creepy contact was able to deduce their birthday. For another person, it was information about being a farmer. And for another person, it was who their photographer was—but that's not something that the writer in question wanted to hide.

But there was one writer who scared me with her posts.

Not only did my creepy contact manage to find her home address (because my writer friend posted photos of her mail *showing* her address), but my creepy contact was able to get information about where her children went to school, where she worked, where her husband worked, and everything else needed to make her life a living hell.

Yeah, *scared* is probably not the right word. *Terrified* is getting closer.

I was on the phone as fast as my fingers could dial. "Are you near your computer? Because we need to lock your account down. Now!" All I had to do was tell her the information about her children, and whoosh . . . She was at the computer, and we were doing what we had to do to sanitize her accounts. I talked her through the process, and we had that baby locked down tighter than a drum within a matter of minutes.

What was more frightening was that she knew she had made mistakes with what she had posted to her account. She *thought* everything was listed as private. The moment I pointed out that her children's safety was at risk, I got zero arguments from her about changing her security settings and cleaning up her account.

DANGER EXISTS NOT JUST ON SOCIAL MEDIA

While I was writing my assassin thriller, I went on the hunt for a quiet little American town that would be unsuspecting if a killer (or two) was in their midst. I started scouring the holiday home sites. I was looking for something unique. I found it in the township of Manzanita, Oregon.

Normally on holiday home listings, you have no idea exactly where the house is located until you make the booking. On this particular listing, the owner had included the street name in the title. In one of the photos was a plaque with the street number nailed to the tree. Bring up Google Earth, and the address of the house was confirmed.

For the writer in me, this little holiday home listing was a gold mine, because I had a full set of photos of the interior and exterior to work from, and the pinpoint location on Google

Earth gave me a map of the surrounding area and other features that I was able to bring into my story.

However, if I was a bad guy intent on doing some harm—casing a joint to burgle—that holiday home listing would have been a prime target.

GPS Check-in Features are as Bad

I know a few people who frequently travel, and whenever they're away, those GPS check-in features tell me where in the world they are. While I love seeing those holiday photos, I also know that they are announcing to the world that they're out of town and that their house and belongings are now ripe for the picking by thieves. And what's worse, in the event of a burglary, their contents insurance won't cover them.

There is a social media clause in a lot of policies for contents insurance. If you post on social media that you're on holiday, your contents insurance is null and void for the duration that you're away.

Are you starting to see why what we post is actually more dangerous than the site's security settings?

In general, for your physical safety, it's not a good idea to advertise your daily location on social media—people don't need to know that information. However, sometimes it's unavoidable.

Things like book signings need to be made public, but if you are taking a box of books to the signing, remove the labels on the boxes. You have no idea who might be snooping around that box when you aren't looking. There is no need to provide that snoopy by-stander with your personal details.

I recommend you turn off the GPS check-in features within social media, but if you really feel the need to use them, do so on departure from a given location. And if you are in the process of moving house, don't post GPS check-ins at any point during the move. It's an invitation to some shady person to go to either address and get sticky-fingered with your possessions.

Be cautious of apps that demand to know your location. For things like your weather app, it might be desirable for them to have this information, but there is absolutely no need for Candy Crush to know this detail.

WE ALL MAKE MISTAKES

Nobody is perfect. Even my own feeds probably have a little too much information about my personal life. Hell, I've had to sanitize my own feeds because of images I posted in my excitement in my younger years when I was still new to this whole social media thing.

I'm not trying to scare anyone into disappearing from the internet world altogether, because I believe that would be career suicide—for both you and me. No, all I want to do is to encourage people to start thinking before they post those photos and other details.

Do you really need to share every aspect of your life? Does that image contain *any* information that could lead to a living nightmare if it found the wrong hands?

I write fiction stories where the bad guy uses the internet and social media to stalk his victims. It might be fiction in my head, but somewhere in the world, a *real* bad guy is doing just that. Don't make it easy for them.

7

THE INTERNET CAN BE FUN TOO

I KNOW THAT I'VE been filled with doom and gloom so far. And I know that there is a lot more doom and gloom to come. But don't be afraid of the internet. The opportunities it can provide are amazing.

For me, presentation opportunities have stemmed from Facebook, as have ideas for different books. I've managed to get honest feedback from those who won't try to sugarcoat things, and I have those that I communicate with on a regular basis, holding myself accountable for my productivity levels, among other things.

My interactions on Twitter (now known as X) led to my own internet radio show about science, which ran on syndicated networks for nearly 3 years. I also met Dan Koboldt through the platform, who offered me a paid writing gig, eventually leading to publication in *Putting the Science in Fiction* with Writer's Digest Books in 2018.

If it wasn't for the internet (and some awesome podcasts), I would have never discovered the works by some extremely talented writers—works that I frequently recommend to others.

And if it wasn't for the internet, I wouldn't be in business as an editor and writing coach.

We will be diving in and out of the other dangers found on the internet during the rest of this book. At every point, view it as an opportunity to learn what not to do, so you can build a strong online platform safely and wisely.

PART TWO
BUILDING A BRAND

8
WHAT IS BRANDING?

WHEN YOU THINK ABOUT your favorite authors, what ideas do you associate with them? Is there a particular tone or feeling that comes to mind? Any particular image? What about what they write? How do you know that a particular passage is from one of their books?

Building a brand is about building recognition. There's a visual aspect that comes through via the images, colors, and fonts. There's a tonal component that is seen in the nature of the posts and the voice used. And there is an underlying message that highlights what that brand represents.

Because of this, when we see a story written by our favorite authors, we know what sort of ride to expect.

If you were to pick up a Dr. Seuss book, you know that there will be a poetic nature to the writing that is filled with nonsensical words. For the more advanced books, there will also be a moral to the story—often centered around tolerance and acceptance. The accompanying pictures also possess a certain quality to them.

There have been many writers over the years who have tried to emulate Dr. Seuss, recreating his magic. However, we knew that they weren't Dr. Seuss books, not just from the author's name, but because there was some element that wasn't quite right.

This is *branding*. It's that recognition element.

And there is really only one way to build a brand: through consistency.

Your platform might include all the ways in which you interact with your audience, but your branding dictates how those interactions might occur.

Yeah, I know that is a wishy-washy explanation, but let's see if we can dive into this branding idea and look at the various components that make up the whole.

WHO ARE YOU? WHAT DO YOU REPRESENT?

The start of a brand starts with *you* as a person. There will be an underlying tone to everything that you do. This will come from your personality and your values. There will be a reason why you write the things you write, and that needs to come through in your branding.

Start by looking at your writing voice and the way you speak to others. Are you bubbly and always cheery? Are you snarky and constantly making jokes? Are you dark and brooding? Or are you blunt and to the point?

What about any themes? Is there an underlying current to your messages and your stories, something that you are passionate about?

Let's say that you write eco-thrillers. And let's say those eco-thrillers revolve around waterways, be it oceans, rivers, lakes, etc. Your branding will likely include images that focus on water scenes, incorporating dark blues and greens. You might share articles about ocean life. Maybe you include scientific information about the land-to-sea barrier. Your messages could highlight the latest research in these areas.

But maybe you don't write thrillers. Maybe you're a children's writer, but not just any children's writer. Let's say you write stories like Cressida Cowell (*How to Train Your Dragon*). You might venture into the legends from around the world about dragons, showcasing some of the cultures that embrace dragons. Or you might dive into the history of Vikings—making it suitable for the children, of course. And you might share information about local children's events.

Who are you? What do you represent? Those questions might carry indistinct answers, but look deeper. Look at your personal subtext.

WHAT ARE YOUR STRENGTHS? WHAT DO YOU ENJOY?

When building a brand and building a platform, you want to lean into your strengths *and* the activities that you enjoy. Without that joy, you won't gain the proficiency for that activity to become a strength. And without the joy, the passion in your work evaporates.

If you don't enjoy what you're doing, it's going to become a chore and it will eventually show in your work. And if you don't enjoy your work, then why should your followers enjoy it?

Let's look at this by way of example.

When I look at my own strengths, I recognize this innate ability to explain things in a way that everyone can understand. This skill has come from years of trying to explain complex scientific and mathematical concepts to my mother. Not that she wanted to understand all the technobabble, but while I was studying, I would use her as a sounding board. She had a philosophy that couldn't be truer: If I could explain it to her, then I understood the concept and not just the terminology.

I also have years of theater stage work behind me: singing, acting, and dancing on stage since I was six years old. All of those years of stage work have taught me how to project my voice, enunciate my words, and make myself heard in a room filled with people who are more interested in what is happening elsewhere.

Today, I combine these two skills in my work as an editor and writing coach, giving presentations and workshops about the various aspects of writing.

All of my activities, including this book, pull on some aspect of these natural strengths. But those are my strengths.

I *enjoy* looking at technology, trying to figure out how the world around me works. As such, there is a speculative thread that seems to weave through everything I do. The one time I tried to move away from the speculative elements within my fiction writing, my brain rebelled and threw in cloning technologies.

Today, I spend a significant amount of time diving into the technology around us. And because of who I am, I examine the dangerous side of that technology.

How can this technology make my characters' lives a living hell? How can this technology make *my life* a living hell?

Everything I do, both in the fiction and nonfiction space, is centered around the dangers of technology. Even when I dive into fantasy worlds, there is still a focus on the dangers that magic (the technology of fantasy) can create.

When you look at your own strengths and enjoyed activities, think about the things that capture your imagination and make you want to learn more. What topics draw you in? What elements and ideas flow through your own writing and various projects?

Do you have a skill set that you seem to draw on frequently? And how can you incorporate that skill set into generating content for your platform?

YOUR ONLINE ACTIVITIES WILL REFLECT YOUR WRITING

Not all of your online activities will involve you putting words to paper. If your platform includes Instagram or TikTok, your content on those sites will possess images and videos.

We will dive more into the different types of social media later in this book, but for the moment, I want you to understand how even your social media posts will be a reflection of the things you write about. There will be something in the essence of what you post that will be entirely *you*.

From the colors you use on your website, through to the images you share on social media, everything will eventually be connected together. There will be a synergy associated with your book covers. And eventually, people will see a new book from you and they'll just know that it's you.

It is only through consistency that you will build the recognition factor that forms a brand.

SEOH!

SEO stands for Search Engine Optimization. With such a mouthful of a term, it's not surprising that so many people talk about SEO like it's some mysterious secret, like there's some magic answer to move your site to the top of search list.

Here's the truth: It's not magic.

The best way to think about SEO rankings is to think of it as the electronic version of brand recognition. The more you do online, and the more people follow your activities, the higher your SEO ranking.

SEO is the little things that site administrators do to aid search engines, such as Google and Bing, to find a site and its pages. It's a simple concept, but one that causes great confusion, and probably because we always talk about it in abstract terms.

Throughout this book, you will find little hints on how to improve your SEO rankings: like using alt-text in your images and formatting pictures for the intended purpose (which have an impact on page load times . . . which in turn impacts on SEO). But even if you do nothing to target SEO specifically, know that just being consistent in your activities online will help to boost your SEO rankings.

9
THE FORGOTTEN EMAIL

How many times have you looked at an email address or the name attached to it and wondered if a person was real? Be honest. How many times have you looked at an email address and developed preconceived ideas about the person who owned that email address?

Many people don't put much thought into the email address they use for general communications, or the impact that it might have. An email is just an email, right? Wrong!

When I was a PhD student, many of my fellow graduate students were forced to fight with the university for the rights to have an email address that didn't say *student*. We were trying to connect with research groups from around the world, but very few groups took us seriously. It didn't matter that we had been at this game for over five years, some of us nearing ten years. No, because our emails said we were *students*, we didn't warrant the time of day. We would be forced to enlist the assistance of our supervisors, who did nothing but grumble about it because it was our project; we should have been able to make whatever inquiries we felt were necessary to whomever we liked.

Believe it or not, the exact same preconceived judging happens to writers too.

If you were to submit a query to an agent or publisher, do you think they would look upon your submission more favorably if your email address was *JoeBloggs@gmail.com* or *furrybottom@donkeyass.com*? Sure, the *furrybottom* email is from a custom domain, but the name can be a little disrespectful. While that email address might not have much impact on your submission at all, I can almost guarantee that any agent to take you on will comment on the appropriateness of your chosen email.

The appropriateness of your email address for communications is only part of the equation.

Go back and reread *Chapter 4: Emails for Writers*. There are so many things to keep in mind when it comes to managing email accounts.

10
THE PEN NAME CONUNDRUM

WRITERS HAVE BEEN FACED with the dilemma of choosing the perfect name to write under for years.

Historically, female writers took on male sounding names because of societal norms. In more contemporary times, some writers have chosen to write under pseudonyms because of the stigma associated with the genre they write—and they want to protect their loved ones from that stigma. A writer might have a birth name that is similar to a famous writer, so a pseudonym might be necessary to help with that separation. (I know the actor Michael Keen had this issue; his birth name is Michael Douglas.) Pseudonyms are also used to separate the types of stories that one writes (like Nora Roberts and J.D. Robb).

Some writers opt to keep their first name but change their last name. This idea means that during in-person interactions, you are more likely to respond to the name being called.

The reasons for choosing a pen name are wide and varied. And the decision to use a pseudonym instead of your real name (or some variant thereof) is a personal decision that only you, as the writer, can make.

However, deciding on the perfect pen name is not a simple matter of choosing between your real name or a fake one. It's also a question of how many others have that name, what that name is already associated with, and spelling variations.

MY WRITER NAME

For me, I write and publish under a variant of my real name. It was a decision that I made years ago.

When I first started publishing scientific journal papers, I chose to publish under *J. L. Mohr*. All publications had to be under a variant of the name that my qualifications were issued under. However, at the time, the engineering and scientific communities still looked down on female scientists. I wanted to avoid any awkward gender conversations by using a non-gender specific name.

When I shifted into the world of fiction, I chose to stick with my real name, because I was proud of the work I did as a researcher. But *J. L. Mohr* was problematic when it came to building an online presence.

A Google search for *J. L. Mohr* turned up an insane number of profiles. For any writer who was trying to get noticed, choosing a name that everyone else seemed to share wasn't going to help me stand out from the noise.

Knowing the online search issues with *J. L. Mohr*, my search for the perfect pen name progressed to every possible combination I could think of that would be some variant of my real name, including typical nicknames and other spelling variations: Judy Mohr; Judith Mohr; Lynn Mohr; Lynne Mohr; Lynette Mohr; J. Lynne Mohr. I think the only variation that I didn't try was using *Moore* instead of *Mohr;* regardless of how common Mohr was, Moore was more so.

But I struck gold when I finally tried *Judy L. Mohr*. The results were all *me.* Every profile that came up, every page found, were pages that were connected to my life as a researcher. From there, I went about building my online presence, starting with social media (namely Twitter and Facebook at the time) and purchasing my custom domain.

Today, if you were to run a Google search for *Judy L. Mohr*, the first four pages of returned results are all me, linking to my various online profiles, my websites, and random articles written in various corners of the web.

It all started with making a decision on what name I wanted to use as a writer.

PURPOSE OF ACCOUNT DICTATES THE USERNAME

Security is always in the forefront of my mind when I sign up for new accounts. But before I get caught up with the site's security settings, I first think about the purpose of the account. The purpose will dictate what email I use in creating that new account, what name I use, what handle I'll attempt to snag, and what sort of interactions I plan to take part in.

I was one of the first users of Facebook when Facebook first went public in 2006. (And for those wondering, while Facebook went live in 2004, it was initially restricted to Harvard students; it became open to the general public in 2006. [1]) I joined the site because I wanted a way to share photos of my kids with the overseas family in the Netherlands and the United States. When I joined all those years ago, it was just my first and last name. At one point, I went through a phase of changing the name on my account to use the same last name as my kids (because of the number of people who got confused as to why my kids had a different last name to me—even though I'm married). Now my activities on Facebook are primarily the writer me, so I've gone back to my own last name. It means that those who interact with me under my personal profile don't get confused about the difference in last name with the public page.

Whenever I join another social media site, it's with my social media login email, snagging my favored *@JudyLMohr* handle. (I have yet to come across a social media site where I can't get my favored handle, but no doubt when I become famous, it will happen. We can have our delusions of grandeur, right?)

When I joined my professional organizations, while I still went after my favored *@JudyLMohr* handle, the email address associated with the accounts depended on whether I was joining as the *writer* or the *editor*.

Every account that I have has a purpose, even if the purpose is *squatting on my favored handle.* Remember that a platform is a lot of moving parts that fit together like a puzzle.

MANAGING MULTIPLE PEN NAMES

It is common for writers to write under multiple pen names. More often than not, it has to do with a writer writing in multiple genres or subgenres, separating the readership for different series. It is entirely up to you whether you choose to write under multiple pen names or keep everything under just the one.

Before you go rushing off to create multiple pen names, I need to remind you that each pen name often requires its own online presence. That means its own social media accounts, its own website, and its own newsletter email list. Though this is not always the case. Some writers have successfully managed to combine their different personas into the same accounts, but it takes careful planning.

If you fall into the multiple-pen-names category, create your platform with intent. Only include the components that you enjoy and will be able to easily maintain. Only sign up for the accounts that will benefit you and your writing. Everything else is noise.

REFERENCES FOR THIS CHAPTER

[1] Wikipedia. (accessed: November, 2023) *History of Facebook.* https://en.wikipedia.org/wiki/History_of_Facebook

11

DOMAIN NAMES ARE NOT EQUAL

ALL WRITERS NEED A website (we'll come back to this argument later). So, because all writers need a website, all writers eventually need to think about their domain names.

You might be in a situation where you have a free subdomain, which might look like *writername.wordpress.com* or *siteprovider.com/username*. Or you might be in a position where you can have a custom domain, like *writername.com*. Regardless of what your website URL is, that address is your internet home. It's an address where people can find you.

The added bonus of a custom domain is that it's an address you can take with you when you move house.

But choosing a domain name is almost as important as choosing the name under which you'll publish. It's not something you should rush into.

Like your pen name, your domain needs to reflect who you are. Your website will form the main portal to your personal brand, so you want to ensure that you choose wisely.

There are many schools of thought about what makes a good domain name.

DOMAINS BASED ON PEN NAME

As writers, we are more than just our stories and characters. If we manage to get a best seller under our belts, then a series or character will become synonymous with our names. What if you want to write a whole new series or develop a different character? Everything is still you.

Shouldn't you encourage the readers of one series to fall in love with another series?

The best way to do that is to showcase your full body of work on the one site. Hence, domain names based on your pen name are the best choice from a long-term marketing perspective.

Consider the following:

The fictitious company Black Feather is starting up to sell glass beads that happen to have feather designs in them. They want to set up a website to sell their products online. (If anyone is actually doing this, please let me know. I would gladly buy some to make myself a nice set of earrings.)

They can set up a website using the domain of *glassfeatherbeads.com*, but their company name is actually Black Feather. Eventually, they want to make other designs, possibly some jewelry too. To allow for growth, they instead choose the name *blackfeatherbeads.com* (simply because *blackfeather.com* is already taken by a wilderness adventure company).

For a writer, *you* are the business; your pen name is your company name. As a consequence, it's vital for your future works that you choose a domain name that will easily allow you to grow.

However, that growth as a writer might come from more than just your books. There might be something else you do that helps build your platform that is just as important. Linking a domain name to a particular book or series would exclude any activities that you might have that are unrelated to writing.

Domains Based on Quirky Nicknames

This one works well for those who want to start a blog with a unique spin.

Example: There are many blogs out there that will review books and interview authors. Almost too many of them. However, there is one where all the interviews are written from the perspective of the protagonist (or antagonist) in the book. While reading these interviews, you quickly get a feel for the tone of the book itself and learn some of the behind-the-scenes thinking that went into writing that book. The blog in question is called *The Protagonist Speaks* (theprotagonistspeaks.com). It's a WordPress.com site, making full use of the free options in a quirky way.

Others will select domain names based on an idea that has become a running theme throughout everything they do, including their logos and images. Sally might have a fascination with red shoes; hence, her domain name would become *sallysredshoes.com* or something like it.

You might not want to market yourself as a writer. Maybe you're a chef, so you might pick a domain name that's related to food and cooking. Saying that, even Gordon Ramsay uses a custom domain based on his name (gordonramsay.com).

Domains Based on a Title

If you have a very successful series, this idea holds a level of merit. In fact, if you intend to only ever write the one story, never once deviating from the one character set, then it makes all the sense in the world.

Many writers of children's stories will do this, because their readers are more likely to remember the series title.

Consider Berenstain Bears. Most people are familiar with this well-loved children's series, but not many people know that it was originally written by Stan and Jan Berenstain, but is now written by Mike Berenstain. Regardless, all the books, games, and other goodies can be found on the one site: berenstainbears.com

However, for those writers who write stories with different characters in different worlds, and are working on multiple series, then having a domain for each series is not only a costly exercise (domain name for each), but a time-consuming one. It involves multiple websites that require constant updating.

*.COM OR WHAT?

Back when the internet was still new, the extensions applied to domains were restricted to *.com (for companies), *.org (for non-profit organizations), *.edu (for educational institutions), and *.gov (for government agencies). But now the list also includes extensions that identify the country, and within each country, there are variations for company, educational, and government sites.

You don't even need to specify the type of organization anymore, either. One of the writing organizations within New Zealand, known as SpecFic New Zealand, has the domain of specfic.nz

If you are looking at the array of options for custom domains, trying to narrow it down for yourself, here are a few things to consider.

What is your primary activity?

Writers at this point are looking at eventually publishing and having their books out there, earning them money. And the moment that money becomes part of the discussion, you are running a company.

And if you're a service provider, like an editor, then you are definitely running a company.

Where is your primary audience located?

The suffix of *.com is commonly associated with the USA. This is why many writers (and businesses) have adopted domains that are more regional. However, in some cases, those regional associations can negatively impact on your ability to market properly. If this is the case, then sticking with the historic *.com extension might play in your favor.

What is the cost associated with your chosen suffix?

Some extensions cost more than others for their annual registrations. If you are working to a tight budget, this cost might play a factor on your decisions.

What limitations are imposed on your chosen suffix?

In the past, those using a *.nz suffix were unable to get privacy protection added to their domains. Privacy protection is the feature where your contact details are hidden from the internet on a WHOIS search (more on WHOIS searches in chapter 17). This is not the case anymore, but this issue played a role in the decisions I made when I was first starting.

And some hosting providers won't host websites with certain extensions. This means that your hosting provider options may be limited.

CHANGING DOMAINS

Regardless of the domain name you choose now, domain names can be changed.

Your domain name is your home on the internet, a house that you rent for a contracted time period. You have the right to renew the domain at any time, but should you decide that you don't want that domain anymore, that you want to move house, you can.

Perhaps you started out with a *.com domain, but decide you actually want a *.com.au (the standard for companies in Australia). No big deal. If you really wanted to, you could have both connected to the same site, where one is listed as the primary domain, and the other has a redirection, directing readers to the primary domain.

If you decide to change your domain name at any point, I recommend forwarding your old site to your new one for a given period of time, just like you would put in a forwarding address if you physically moved house. This way, your readers can find your new home.

You might need to update your platform to reflect the current situation, but keep in mind your long-term goals.

12

DREADED PROFILE PHOTOS

IN A WAY, WRITERS are public figures. Like all public figures, you need a profile photo. This one image will be linked to everything that you do.

There are many schools of thought on profile photos. Some insist that you use only a professional head shot. Others say that your profile photo should show you doing something interesting. Others are quite vocal about those common pictures of cats.

Like all aspects of your platform, your profile photo needs to reflect who you are, but it will change as you develop and grow. (It'll change as you get older and grow more wrinkles.) There is no need to pay a fortune for that profile picture. However, there are a few basic guidelines that you should follow.

USE A PHOTO THAT IS UNIQUELY YOU

Ideally, your profile photo should be same across *all* of your social media and website branding. This is *your* mark. As such, you need to ensure that you make the image identifiable as uniquely you.

Sorry, guys, but those random typewriter images are not unique, and neither are those cat pictures. However, if you are not comfortable about having your own photo taken, there are some tricks that you can play.

For years, Lemony Snicket (a.k.a. Daniel Handler) used an image of himself dressed in his trench coat and a fedora, taken in dark shadow. You couldn't see his face or any other identifiable feature of his person. Yet, the image was uniquely him.

Five years ago, Wil Wheaton used a caricature of himself. Again, his physical features were not revealed in that image, but it was still identifiable as Wil Wheaton. Today, on all of his social media, it's a photo of himself drinking from one of his bizarre mugs. Each social media account sports a different mug, but all of those images are uniquely Wil Wheaton.

Is there a distinctive feature about yourself or your writing that is just you? Perhaps you are always seen wearing converse sneakers, even when wearing an evening gown. Or maybe you always have your nose stuck in a book. The options are limitless.

USE A RECENT PHOTO

If you are actually using a picture of yourself, one in which you can see your face, ensure that it's a recent image.

People will go to conferences or other events expecting to see the person in that photo. And when the person who shows up is someone who is significantly older than their profile photo . . . or has lost a significant amount of weight compared to their profile photo . . . or changed their hair color . . .

Let me give you an example of the type of confusion I mean.

Donald Maass (one of the leading literary agents in the world and the author of multiple books for writers) used to use a photo from when he was in his forties. He used that photo for the longest time. The first time I was in a workshop with him, I was confused. The man running the workshop was in his late-sixties.

Donald Maass now uses a photo that is more reflective of what he looks like now, but occasionally, that old profile photo gets used for promotional purposes.

Another way to think of this particular situation is passports photos. Passports need to be renewed ever five to ten years based on your country's requirements. They do this because we age.

Are you getting the hint?

If you have aged significantly since your last profile photo was taken, it might be time to face the camera again.

A Photo of Only You

It is important that you are *the only person* in the photo. If you want to use a picture of you with one of your pets, there is nothing wrong with that. It shows off your personality.

Your photo should be one that was taken for the purpose of showing off your best side. Don't use a picture that was taken at someone's wedding and cropped. Seeing someone's arm draped around your shoulders is distracting.

The only exception to this is when it's a profile photo for a writing duo or group.

Image Backgrounds

There are some industry professionals who insist that your profile image should be taken on a white background, and that you need to be wearing dark clothing, so your shoulders don't disappear into the background. This may have been the case in the past when everything was in printed form only, as it decreased the amount of color needed for that image. Today, however, a significant amount of publishing is in electronic form and your profile photo is likely to be seen on a color screen.

Wear whatever you want and have that photo taken wherever you want, as long as it shows off your personality.

Avoid a *busy* background. I'm talking about something with a lot of things going on behind you. A photo with you leaning against the tree could be great, but if there's a playground filled with kids in the background, that could be too much.

Avoid Fancy Filters

I also recommend against using fancy filters. Many smartphones give you the ability to overlay stars or bunny ears onto your photos. While this might be cute, your profile photos still need to look professional. Unless your branding deliberately incorporates bunny ears or dog noses, don't use them.

Image Sizes

Whatever you choose, ensure that the image is identifiable as *you* even when seen in tiny icon mode. Sorry, guys, but those memes might look good in large scale, but they're deplorable when seen as a small icon.

Ensure that the resolution of the image is suitable for all media and with all cropping sizes that might be applied.

Profile images used within most social media sites tend to be 250 x 250 pixels square; however, some sites want 500 x 500 pixels square. Some sites want 800 x 800 circles. However, those sites will create the circles for you.

To make your life easy, you'll want to have an image that is of a reasonable size and clarity when using a high-quality printing resolution of 300 – 600 dpi (dots per inch). Images taken using your smartphone camera might be insufficient for this purpose. It depends on what mode you used when taking those photos on your smartphone and what quality of camera you have.

We'll go deeper into the pixel resolutions needed for your photos when we take a deep dive into websites, but for now, know that you need to have a file on hand that is in the order of 1800 x 1800 pixels at a minimum for that high-resolution 6-inch photo. Larger photos (promo banners) require significantly more pixels.

13
BIOS
ONE SIZE WON'T FIT ME

WRITERS ARE HAPPY TO dive into those fictional worlds with fire-breathing dragons or steamy encounters with that dark knight. However, as comfortable as wc are with our imaginations, there is one topic that many writers struggle to write about: ourselves.

It's ironic . . . Here we are, words flow easily on the page when discussing some fictional character, but writing about the one person that we know the best . . . You have got to be kidding.

However, writing a bio is not something a writer should shy away from. There are many ways to spin what might seem like the boring hum-drum of life, making it sound glamorous. We're writers. We can do this, right?

Any bio, even the bios on our *About* pages of our websites, should be able to answer four key questions.

1) What do you write?
2) What drives you to do what you do?
3) What are some of your accomplishments?
4) What else do you do?

Let's look at this one question at a time.

WHAT DO YOU WRITE?

Your bio needs to tell us about what you write. What genre? What themes? Any messages that you seem to focus on?

It's perfectly acceptable to admit that you write a wide range of stories that span across multiple genres. You might be a person with diverse ideas that seem to burst forth all at once. But regardless if you write cross-genres or stick to a single genre, we need to know what section of the bookstore (digital or brick-and-mortar) that we might find your writing in.

If you write stories about diversity or cultural differences, your bio needs to reflect that.

If you write other stories under a different pseudonym, you might want to include that here. Then again, if your website is for a writer of children's stories, you might not want to mention that you also write erotica under the pen name of Dusty Hole. *No offense to Miss Hole.*

WHAT DRIVES YOU TO DO WHAT YOU DO?

Where do you draw inspiration from? Do you have a background in something relevant to your writing? This is your chance to show others why only you can write the stories that you do.

If you have a background in something relevant to what you write, include it. You might be a history major writing fiction which takes place during the French Revolution. Or maybe you have a science degree, and your stories often have a science fiction bent. (Guilty!)

You don't need an entire essay to answer this; you should be able to sum it up into a few words.

For me, I just love to be swept away into the world of my imagination; sometimes, I refuse to resurface.

WHAT ARE SOME OF YOUR ACCOMPLISHMENTS?

Include any special mentions for your published works. If you are still waiting to see your name in print, mention that award-winning fish that you caught and turned into an awesome meal that wasn't burnt.

Okay, maybe not that last one, but there is always a way to turn the hum-drum into the exciting.

This brings me to the next question.

WHAT ELSE DO YOU DO?

Being a writer is one thing. Being a writer who enjoys getting lost in the forest while hunting deer is something entirely different—especially if those deer keep threatening to hunt you in return.

You don't need to include an entire expose about your life, but it is a good idea to remind your readers that you're not some artificial intelligence program that can win literary awards. (Think I'm joking about that one? Look it up. I was shocked to see it.)

CRAFTING A BIO: START WITH AN INTERVIEW

The art of writing a bio comes down to the answers to the four questions above—and not necessarily the serious answers. I have written many bios over the years, some for myself and some for clients of Black Wolf Editorial Services.

Often clients feel self-conscious talking about themselves. Frequently, I encounter those who feel ashamed to admit that they don't do much outside of their main job or the writing. When I interview them, often something little is said, seemingly insignificant. But it's the little things that can become nuggets of gold, making your bio stand out from the rest.

Let me give you an example.

One client said to me that she sometimes fidgets with paper and folds origami. It was a side comment, but it found its way into the final version of her bio.

> *"An engineer by day, and gamer when time allows, this paper ninja writes, reads and plays with pen-and-paper RPGs and folds origami. It's not surprising that her stories are filled with unexpected folds and twists that blend seamlessly with reality."*

The irony in this: that writer has now formed her entire branding around that one throwaway comment. Origami swans and throwing stars are everywhere on her website and on her social media. Even her newsletter includes the origami gems.

If you are really struggling to think of what you should include in your bio, have a friend interview you, taking notes of your conversation. Even the newest of writers have those little quirks that make them interesting people.

Bio Voice

Bios are often written in third person—especially bios included in press kits or at the end of publications.

It's odd to think of yourself in the third person, but bios are used as an introduction of sorts. If it helps, pretend that you are writing about someone you only just met.

Any bios written in first person belong on your website or in articles where you are talking about yourself and your experience. You might even be tricky and use a first person variant on your social media (where there are no rules).

But in all cases, your bio needs to capture the essence of who you are, why you write what you write, and the things that are unique to you.

STRUCTURE OF A BIO

Depending on how your online platform is structured, you may have multiple variants of the same bio: a micro-bio for use on social media profiles; the short bio for use on sites like Goodreads and Amazon; and a longer bio to include on your personal website.

All variants of your bio will contain similar elements, but the emphasis will be tailored for the specific use.

The structure of a bio, regardless of its length, should follow the same pattern:

- what you do, i.e., writer of whatever genre and any other key activities;
- why you do it, serious or not;
- key accomplishments, if you have room; and
- other activities that prove you're human.

Notice that this order is the same as the questions above. There is a reason for that.

Bios will also include call-to-action elements. Call-to-action statements are your marketing statements, but not worded like a pushy used-car salesman. They're subtle—hook and entice. Exactly which call-to-action elements are used will depend on where the bio is being shown.

So, how does one get all of this information into the bios of varying lengths?

MICRO-BIOS

The micro-bio is what you will find on various social media sites. The length of it will depend on the site itself.

Most sites allow for bios of 80 to 150 characters in length (including spaces). Some platforms allow for a longer bio or page description, but to be the most effective, you want to keep your bios on social media to something short and catchy. Use incomplete sentences and take advantage of punctuation.

Let's take a look at my micro-bios.

On Instagram and Threads:

Kiwi Judy L Mohr is a #writer, freelance #editor, and science geek. Check out her crazy adventures.

Sites like Instagram and X allow you to put hashtags and other links in your micro-bios, but don't use too many. The eyes glance over links, hunting out text (and hashtags render as links).

And be aware that whatever you use on Instagram will be filtered through to Threads, because the two profiles are linked. However, at the time of writing this book, hashtags within bios didn't work on Threads.

On Facebook:

Writer, editor, writing coach, amateur photographer, mother & wife. So many ways to get into trouble.

On LinkedIn:

Writer, Developmental Editor, Writing Coach, & Just Plain Crazy

The exact wording used within micro-bios will show elements of your personality, hence why in my micro-bios, I've included statements like "crazy adventures", "so many ways to get into trouble", or "just plain crazy". And each micro-bio is tailored for the platform they are listed on.

For more examples, look at the bios of the accounts that you follow on your social media of choice.

Short Bios

The limitation on the short bio is defined by those "See More" links on sites such as Goodreads and Amazon. Most people don't bother to click those links, so anything that doesn't show in the first few lines tends to go sight unseen. For those who do click on the "See More" links . . .

How many times have you done just that, only to discover that it was only one or two more words to the bio? Grr! Frustrating!

Writers, why, oh why, would you ever want to have your precious words that you spent such a long time crafting to go unseen by the masses? Sorry, guys, but you need to pull out that editing hat and edit the crap out of that bio, so it fits within the spaces allowed.

Most of these bios are restricted to approximately 40 words. However, this is not an exact measure, as it will depend on the number of lines that those 40 words take up on the website in question.

Your short bio is typically the one used for guest blogging, presentations, and interviews. Of all the bio variants that you might have, it will be your short bio (or some version of it) that gets used the most.

While the micro-bio is often missing the call-to-action elements, because of how often your short bio will be used, those call-to-action elements will be vital.

Let's take a look at my short bio.

Kiwi Judy L Mohr is a writer, developmental editor, and a science nerd with a keen interest in internet technologies and social media security. Her knowledge ranges from highly efficient ways to hide the bodies through to how to improve your SEO rankings for your website. When she isn't writing,

> *editing, or doing something for writing within the local community, she can be found plotting her next foray into mischief and scouting for locations to hide the bodies. (Shh . . . Don't tell anyone.) You can follow her crazy adventures on her blog (judylmohr.com) or on Instagram (@JudyLMohr).*

A version of this particular short bio can also be found on Goodreads, Gravatar, Facebook (*About::Details about you* section), LinkedIn, and everywhere else where a bio is included as part of the account profile. I also use this bio (or a variant thereof) for guest blogs and interviews.

Notice how my short bio finishes with a call-to-action: an invitation to visit my personal website or follow me on social media.

In general, your bios are going to be similar on all sites, but they will also be slanted in a way that suits the site they are listed on. As such, have a generic short bio (included as part of your press kit on your website) that you tailor and edit for each specific site, so it fits within the limits allowed.

(We will dive deeper into the press kit later.)

MEDIUM AND LONG BIOS

The bio on your website will be an expanded version of your short bio, adding a few more quirky details. If you have more than one site (as I do), ensure that the emphasis of the bio is slanted toward the purpose of the site that it appears on.

The length of a long bio shouldn't be any longer than one to two scrolls of the page. If you have written so much that you need to scroll down five times to see the full bio on a desktop/laptop screen, then that bio may need to be edited. (Many readers won't read past two scrolls deep.)

This longer bio will most likely only ever appear on your website. So, there is no need to turn it into an essay of its own. Instead, this is the time to let your personality shine through.

But there are a few special bios that we should also mention.

BIOS FOR QUERYING

For those who are looking at submitting to agents or publishers, the bio section of your query letter is an entirely different beast to the bios presented above.

In this case, your bios will be of a short bio variant, but written in first person, focusing on your accomplishments and qualifications. You don't bother with the answers to Questions 1 or 4 from above, and your answer to Question 2 should be restricted to only those aspects that are directly related to the project you are querying.

Only mention what you do for a day job if it has direct relevance to your story. If you don't have any publication credits, just stay silent about it. However, do mention any memberships that you have to writing organizations or big conferences that you have attended. They show your dedication to writing.

Just so you can get an idea of what I'm talking about, the following is the bio that I used back when I first starting querying in 2015, back when I had zero writing credits to speak of, but I was active in the writing community.

> *I'm a member of the Christchurch Writers' Guild and SpecFic New Zealand. I'm also an active member of the Scribophile online writing community, and have recently been appointed the NaNoWriMo Municipal Leader for my region.*

And the bio that went out with queries in 2022 was as follows.

> *I'm a public speaker and advocate for online safety. I'm a contributor to* 'Putting the Science in Fiction', *published by Writer's Digest in 2018, and was awarded an Honorable Mention in L. Ron Hubbard's Writers of the Future Contest 2nd Quarter 2020. I was also a quarter-finalist in the*

> *ScreenCraft Cinematic Book Competition for 2022. I'm a member of the New Zealand Society of Authors, Australian Crime Writers' Association, and Sisters in Crime.*

I need to highlight that the comment about being a public speaker and advocate for online safety was only included in this particular query bio because the manuscript in question centered around a bad guy who finds his victims via social media. Other manuscripts that I was querying at the time excluded this line.

Bios for Service Providers

Everything above is targeted at bios for writers and other creatives. They are focused on you and your activities. However, for service providers, a bio that focuses entirely on you is not going to help you land that next contract.

When people come to your website seeking your services, they aren't interested in your qualifications directly. They want to know how you can help them.

This creates a shift in the paradigm included in crafting a bio.

A bio for a service provider needs to answer the following questions:

1) What experience do you have, highlighting that you understand your client's needs?
2) What benefits will a client get if they work with you?
3) What steps are involved in starting that process?
4) What sort of experience can they expect working with you?

Notice that there is no mention of qualifications. And when you discuss your experience, it needs to be phrased in such a way that it's relatable to the client. They want to know that in hiring you, you will understand what they are going through.

But even the small amount that is about you (your experience) is still not about you. It's about what you can do for your client.

Showcase your personality and your general approach to doing things. Give prospective clients that initial taste of what they can expect from you.

Variants of my own service provider bios can be found on my *Meet the Editor* page on Black Wolf Editorial Services (blackwolfeditorial.com/about) and on my directory listing on the Editorial Freelancers Association website (www.the-efa.org/memberinfo/judy-mohr-33753).

Final Comments About Bios

I know that's a lot of information to absorb. Just remember that you are a writer, and as a writer, you have the skills needed to make your bio glitter like gold.

If you are using this book as a guide, building your online platform as you read through this book, then take the time to write your various bios. Send them to your writing buddies for input and critique. And remember to incorporate your personality.

To help you with your bios, I have created a little worksheet to remind you of the key elements of the micro, short, and longer bios. You can access the bios handout and all other supplementary materials for this book at:

blackwolfeditorial.com/hidden-traps-book

14

IS YOUR PROFILE A TURNOFF?

PUBLISHING HAS ALWAYS BEEN a *business*, and writers are expected to build *brands*, which consist not only of the books they write but also of their social media and online presence. Our non-writing activities have always been a part of this whole marketing thing, and how we handle that message is just part of the game. However, the internet has added a *now* component to the marketing equation that wasn't there before, and disaster is waiting to happen.

Whatever the issue is at hand, everyone has an opinion on it, even if that opinion is, "Whatever . . . Don't care."

Some people are super excited to share their opinions with the world, and this trait is admirable. We should be able to express our opinions and thoughts in a public forum. But it doesn't take much to spark the fires of the lynch mob.

The real problem with the way social media works is that *mob psychology rules the internet*. If the mob thinks that what you have said is inappropriate, there is no back pedaling and taking those comments back. The damage is done. Your reputation is now food for the wolves.

It doesn't matter if the mob is completely wrong on the topic. It doesn't matter if you are the expert in the field with all the facts and figures behind you. All that matters is that you have an opinion that differs from what the lynch mob thinks. And that lynch mob can actually be quite small—just incredibly vocal.

If you search the internet, you'll find countless number of topics that have sparked the fires. And you can find example after example of a comment going viral and damaging a person's reputation.

Case in point: Roseanne Barr and her supposedly sarcastic tweet that led to the cancellation of her new show in late 2018.

But there are underlying currents on social media that can drag an unsuspecting writer under, and they never resurface. There are certain threads and certain movements that have sprouted up over the years that public figures have chosen to get behind and support. Some have been great, and some of them . . . Well . . .

Remember that it is mob psychology that rules the internet. It doesn't matter if you are right or wrong. If the mob believes it should be one way, then anything you say or do is only fuel for those fires and will likely come back and bite you in the ass—especially if your comments or actions go against the masses.

There are two topics in particular that are incredibly sensitive topics, but they are also topics that seem to weave through everything that we do.

I'm referring to politics and religion.

(And this is where I, myself, need to be incredibly careful—in case the mob wants to attack me.)

DOES YOUR PLATFORM REVOLVE AROUND POLITICS OR RELIGION—AND YOU DON'T KNOW IT?

I'm *not* a political person. I actually despise politics. In fact, I go out of my way to avoid politics, particularly on the internet. And I'm private about my spirituality and religious practices. There are certain things that some people just don't need to know.

Ironically, offline and in person, I'm highly opinionated and not afraid to have those emotional debates and heated conversations. But noticed I said offline and in person. That is the vital part of this situation.

When you are talking to people in person, you can take clues from body language, giving you the opportunity to defend yourself when things get a little out of control. The conversation might become a little heated, but you are often in the position where you can back pedal a bit and rephrase your argument in a way that gets heard.

However, on social media, and on the internet in general, once it's out there, you can *never* take it back. To make matters worse, there is absolutely no way of knowing for certain what will send the mob into full-attack mode.

On social media, I'm hyper-aware of any statement that might be seen as political or religious in nature. I do what I can to stay under the radar. Yet, even I've fallen prey to the mob—more than once.

Because of the super-charged politically correct environment that we live in today, almost anything can be taken as being political or religious—even the color of your toothbrush. And that smiley face emoji can have other meanings too.

Who else can recall the teenage girl who was publicly attacked for wearing a Chinese-style dress to her prom? It was an innocent photo, yet the public still attacked her for cultural appropriation.

And I had a writing buddy who had her Twitter account (as it was known back then) suspended because she shared a photo of the commissioned artwork she had done of a bald eagle soaring through the sky holding the American flag in its talons. Someone decided that the artwork was a form of cruelty to animals rather than the patriotic symbol that it was. Thankfully, she managed to get that one overturned, because it almost took her away from social media altogether. Some people . . . *I really wish there was a rolling eyes emoji that worked in all book formats.*

Understand Your Audience

I mentioned that commissioned artwork for a reason, and it wasn't just to make a point about how even the innocent can send the mob after you. I mentioned it, because when posting things on your public feeds, you need to think about the type of reader you're trying to attract.

My writing buddy, the one with the bald eagle artwork, is deliberately trying to attract military and patriotic readers. She writes military thrillers, and those who come from military backgrounds or who are patriotic themselves would most likely enjoy her stories. Besides, I swear that woman bleeds red, white, and blue.

Would I put something like that on my personal feed? Hell no! But that is *not* the type of reader that I'm trying to attract.

I tend to share things about science and technology—the good, the bad, the dangerous, and the hilarious. I share tidbits about the things I'm learning about forensics and other research that finds my stories. I even share the odd picture that I find funny.

I'm a parent who is frustrated with her young adult children, but I also understand the importance of teaching them how to be safe on the internet.

And of course, I share what I can about developmental editing.

It's about trying to attract the right kind of reader to build *my* audience.

STEPS TO ATTRACT THE RIGHT AUDIENCE

Here are a few quick steps to help attract the right audience to your feeds.

1) Identify your target audience.

The first step in any of this is to identify your target audience, and get specific. It's all well and good to say that you write fantasy, but what kind of fantasy? What kind of romance, if that's what you're writing? There is a whole spectrum out there.

Exactly who is your reader? Describe them.

If your reader is exactly like you, then what type of person are you? If your readers are children who are like your own children, then describe your children!

For me, the ideal reader for my personal writing is going to be happy to rough and tumble it in the mud, but will occasionally like getting cleaned up. They will not be afraid of the blood and guts (even if they do faint at the sight of blood), and they will be a bit of a science geek. They will also know that life doesn't always work out exactly how they intended.

Guess what, people: I just described myself.

2) Craft your bios to highlight the parts of yourself that your target audience can relate to.

Almost every single iteration of my personal bio out there highlights the fact that I enjoy being outdoors with my family and that I'm into science. This is part of the makeup of my target audience, so why would I hide that from the world?

If you write Christian fiction, then wouldn't it be a good idea to highlight the fact that you're Christian? Or maybe I'm overthinking this.

3) Share things on your feeds that your target audience would actually like.

It might seem obvious, but if your target audience prefers reading your cleverly crafted murder mysteries, why are you sharing those posts about the latest Jane Austen retelling that's been released? (And we shall not discuss that beyond-laughable disaster known as *Pride and Prejudice and Zombies.*)

4) Pick your battles.

This one is really about protecting your platform and reputation, but keeping your target audience in mind.

There is always some hot topic on the news. Don't comment on everything that gets you hot under the collar. There are some things that would be better if you just kept it to yourself and your offline life. However, if something topical blends right into your platform and your target audience would enjoy it, then go for it.

For me, that will be anything that I encounter about internet security and advanced technology.

With all the security issues that Facebook has faced over the years, I've gotten more than just a little vocal, constantly reminding people to examine their security settings and to assess their posting behavior. Come on, even this book is connected to that topic.

Do you see where I'm going with this?

5) Be true to yourself.

With your activities on social media, you are playing a part, but you also need to be somewhat true to who you are in real life.

If you despise a situation, then don't go online saying it's okay—because it's not okay! If you're a sarcastic fool who is often cracking jokes, then let the humor fly. And if punctuation and grammar are your thing, then go for it. Just don't take offense if I happen to disagree with you on something.

6) Don't be afraid of the trolls.

The people who get you and your work will actually rally around you. They will help provide that wall against the trolls.

That said, *never* let your support network attack someone on your behalf. Word of that particular behavior will spread and come back to bite you in the ass.

But when you are feeling particularly low, your support network will help to pick you up again.

Hell, if you need to, reach out to me via Mastodon, Facebook, or through my websites, and I'll send you the virtual hug that you so desperately need. For that matter, you could contact me on Instagram, though I don't tend to respond to private message requests there for a variety of reasons, too lengthy to go into now.

As long as you are smart about what you are posting, keeping your target audience in mind, social media and online activities can be a lot of fun and highly rewarding. The opportunities to succeed are endless—as long as you learn how to play the game.

PART THREE
THE MUST-HAVE WEBSITE

15

ALL WRITERS NEED A WEBSITE

WHEN THE INTERNET FIRST became common back in the late 1990s, creating a website required many long laborious hours of coding just to get one page looking the way it should. Today, anyone can have a website; anyone can have a blog. Writers don't need to stress ourselves with HTML, CSS coding, or JavaScript. (Not that many writers even know what these are.) Instead, we can focus on the page content and get it out there.

However, this new, easy-to-use playground has meant that there is a new expectation of writers that no previous generation has had to contend with before. As writers who wish to be published, traditionally or indie-published, we have to have a website of our own.

THE IMPORTANCE OF A WEBSITE

If there is only one thing that you do in building an online presence, then your focus should be on your website.

Prospective readers will go to your website to get the latest information about your various projects, both old and new. You will likely have a list of all your published books, links to where they can be purchased, and links to interviews and other little goodies. Yes, your social media will likely have information about the latest happenings. However, any older material will quickly be buried.

Everything else you do online should point back to your website. It's the one central hub where readers can get the most up-to-date information about your work.

Let me say that again.

> Your website will have the most up-to-date information about your work. This means that you *need* to keep it up to date!

I can't stress this point enough. If you're a writer seeking to be published and to actually sell your books, you need a website.

There will be some out there who say that they don't worry about things such as websites because they let their agent or publisher do it for them. Umm . . . These people are already published with an established readership.

If you're just starting out, you need to do it yourself. You won't have an agent, publisher, or publicist to help you. You're it, baby!

If you're lucky, after you obtain a publication contract, you might get some help and advice on what to do, but there is no guarantee. In many cases, publishers want to see that you are already active in this area, planning to tap into whatever following you have amassed on your own to sell your books. It is cruel of the industry to leave new writers to flounder around on their own, but that's the way of the current internet world.

And for those wanting to indie-publish, your website will be the most important aspect of your marketing tool set.

But all hope is not lost. A writer's platform is ever-changing.

Don't feel that you have to get the website design perfect from the word go. It will evolve as you evolve. You'll expand your ideas, and your website will need to expand as a consequence. Elements might remain constant, such as the domain name, but there will be times when you feel the need to reinvent yourself.

Nothing you do is cast in stone.

So, where does one begin?

When looking to start your own website, there are many things that you should consider.

ABILITY TO GROW

At all times, keep in mind your long-term goals. I'm not suggesting that you should build your website for that long-term goal. Definitely not. You should build your website for your current situation, but with the ability to grow.

This simple growth concept might decide your course of action to start, but in case it doesn't, here are a few other things that you'll want to consider.

COST

Most writers are poor. More often than not, we need to hold down another job to put food on the table and a roof over our heads. Even those with many published books under their belts tend to struggle to make ends meet from book sales alone.

Take a good look at your favorite authors. Look at the other things that they need to do to bring in the money. Writing is only part of it.

For those writers who are just starting out, any financial decision needs to be weighed carefully. The word *free* is very attractive. And in the world of websites, *free* is actually a good starting option. Back in 2010, a free website would have looked cheap, but that's not the case today.

Today, there are a number of providers advertising *free* websites and all the tools you need to get your site up and operational quickly. They offer a variety of themes and are user-friendly. With a society that has come to love their internet-based communications, affordable and user-friendly is a must.

WEBSITE, BLOG, OR A COMBINATION?

There will be some writers out there who will see the word *blog* and will start to panic. Some writers will likely be already freaking out about the idea of needing a website, and the idea of a blog . . .

Let me settle those fears now, so people can stop hyperventilating.

> A website is *not* a blog.

People might believe that the two terms are interchangeable, but they aren't.

A website is your internet home, containing information about yourself and your various projects. The pages are static, occasionally updated to reflect changes. It will contain the most up-to-date information about your work, assuming that you actually keep it up to date.

A blog, on the other hand, is like a diary, constantly changing with whatever content or other information you choose to share with the world. In some respects, a blog will contain even more up-to-date information about your work. However, the information on a blog quickly gets buried, depending on the frequency at which you post new content. This means that you can't rely on your blog as a marketing tool for older works.

If a reader visits your website, they want to be able to find your books, products, or whatever quickly—and with little effort. This is the key point that distinguishes a website from a blog.

And here is where the line blurs.

Many bloggers host their blogs on their websites, either as the home page or as a separate menu item. However, some elect to have a different site constructed to host their blogs separate from their primary site. All are acceptable options, but they serve different purposes.

However, if you really don't want to have a blog, you don't need one. You need a website, yes, but a blog . . . It's a personal preference. Don't let anyone bully you into doing something that you don't want to do. Simple as that!

For the writers who elect to have a blog, I personally feel that you would be better served to have a blog hosted on the same site as your other writing stuff. From an SEO perspective, this will boost activity of a site, increasing SEO rankings. However, make sure that whatever content you include in your blog matches the primary purpose of your site.

If it's a business site, then keep the content professional and your rants somewhere else. (This is part of the reason why I have two blogs myself.)

I will go deeper into blogging in *PART 4: Mountain of Blog*.

Custom Design?

Your website is your home on the internet. This means that you want to make that home reflect who you are as the writer. Everything on the site—the colors, the fonts, the images, the content—all need to fit within your chosen branding.

If you don't have the ability to change the look and feel of the pages, then the theme associated with that website (or hosting provider) will not service your needs.

Ease of Obtaining a Custom Domain

When starting out, it's perfectly okay to get a *free* website with a subdomain of whatever provider you use. A subdomain commonly uses the format of *writername.siteprovider.com* or *siteprovider.com/username*. But eventually, you will want a custom domain.

We've already covered the importance to your branding of choosing the right domain name back in chapter 11. But now we need to think about whether we can have that custom domain or not.

If you are using a self-hosted site, you will have that custom domain from word go. However, for the free sites, it might be possible to get a custom domain mapped to your free site. In some cases, those *free* website providers require that you upgrade to a business plan, but not always.

WordPress.com, in particular, gives the option to include a custom domain on a free website (costing you only the price of the domain registration). They bury the option, because they want you to pay for the more expensive plans. But their support documentation provides the details on how to do it at:

wordpress.com/support/domains/connect-existing-domain

EASE TO ADD SUBSCRIPTION FORMS

In today's market, you want to have an email newsletter or something like it. Having access to your readers' inbox is incredibly valuable when it comes to marketing new books. We will take a deep dive into newsletters later in this book, but for now, I want you to focus on the integration of the subscription tools into your website.

If you are using a self-hosted site, it will be a matter of finding the right plugin or add-on tool to do the job, connecting to your email list provider using whatever instructions they've given you. But the free websites can be a little more tricky.

Even if you are forced to create a button that will go to an external form, there is always a way to do it. Just make sure that you know what options you have available to you based on your website hosting.

Since we've opened that can of worms about free vs self-hosted sites, let's just take the time to dive deeper into that idea now.

16
FREE OR PAID?

IF YOU'RE NOT SURE exactly what you want to achieve with your website, start with a free one. There is nothing wrong with a *free* website. Using providers like WordPress.com, you can create professional sites with little effort, without it costing you the earth.

Free websites from providers like WordPress.com, Weebly, and Wix all have a few things in common.

All of them have no contracts or fees when starting out. They will allow you to choose a domain name, but they will give you a subdomain URL in the form of *chosenname.provider.com* This is not a bad thing, because at least you are building your brand recognition with your chosen name.

They often use user-friendly page builder tools, though some are more user-friendly than others. And there are often a number of themes that you can choose from for your websites. No technical skills are required to get your website up and going—you just need the content.

However, the free options also possess similar cons too.

The options and resources available for your websites will be limited. For example, Wix and Weebly don't allow you to embed signup forms on your website to external providers. On WordPress.com, you might not be able to have an embedded form, but you can use a popup signup form to common email list providers.

The free sites also tend to offer limited technical support, and they might require you to pay for add-ons or upgrades to become fully usable sites. They will restrict how much customization you have access to, limiting how much of your branding you can incorporate into your site.

And the biggest con: the cost of a free website is the advertising that providers put on your website. Sometimes, you can influence what ads are shown, but more often than not, you can't.

I know I'm sounding a little negative about free sites here, but seriously, they are a good option for newer and emerging writers. I started out on a free website from WordPress.com with a custom domain mapped onto it. If it wasn't for business decisions that I made years ago, I would likely still be using that free website, nearly a decade after it was first created.

OPTIONS FOR FREE WEBSITE HOSTING

To find the right option for you, you need to look at the ease of use, the connectivity of the site with your other social media, the ability to upgrade or go self-hosted in the future, and the overall look and feel of the resulting website. Take a look at other websites using the different providers and see which one gives you the best feeling.

At the time this book was written, the free options that produced usable websites for writers included the following.

- WordPress (wordpress.com)
- Weebly (weebly.com)
- Wix (wix.com)
- Tilda Publishing (tilda.cc)
- Infinity Free (infinityfree.com)

Be careful of providers that say they offer *free* websites for a trial period. The costs associated can be more than you were expecting. SquareSpace, a common host provider among writers, is free for only 14 days. After that, you need to pay.

THE OPTION I RECOMMEND

Personally, of all the free website-building options, I would recommend WordPress (wordpress.com).

Before anyone accuses me of being paid to make an advertisement, I should stress that my recommendation is based on my own personal experience and research.

On the free WordPress.com site, you can map a custom domain onto the site for approximately US$20 per year, depending on the domain suffix, and this includes privacy protection where available. And WordPress sites are highly portable, allowing you to easily move hosting providers (becoming self-hosted in the future), taking all of your content with you. The same can't be said for sites like Weebly or Wix. This ability to grow is a highly attractive feature.

The themes available for free WordPress websites count in the thousands, with many of them being highly customizable.

The first version of my personal website used a free WordPress.com account with a custom domain mapped onto it, and that was back in 2014. WordPress.com has improved its systems significantly since then, making it more customizable and user-friendly.

WHEN TO CHOOSE TO GO SELF-HOSTED

Free websites are a good option for simple websites with minimal traffic. However, there comes a point when *free* just doesn't cut it anymore.

You should consider self-hosted website services if any of the following apply to you.

1) You are a professional service provider (e.g., an editor, a graphic designer, a marketing consultant).
2) You have a lot of pages, files, and content.
3) You want good security or responsive customer support.

4) You are trying to develop your brand for monetization.
5) You are expecting a high amount of traffic to your website.
6) You want full control over your website, including any ads that get listed.

SITES THAT ARE NOT WEBSITES

During my encounters with new writers, many of them will tell me that they have a blog, but not a full-fledged website. When I ask where I can find their blog to take a look, they give me a URL that leads to a social media site.

Except for Tumblr, Medium, and Substack, social media sites should never be thought of as an option for a website or a blog. This includes Facebook, LinkedIn, Pinterest, and other similar social media sites.

Social media sites are intended for networking and reaching out to a fraction of your audience. In most cases, social media sites require readers to have their own account on the site to read your posts.

17

SELF-HOSTING
SHOULD I?

FOR A MOMENT, LET'S assume that you don't want to head down the road of a free website, but rather have a self-hosted site from the word go. Or maybe you're looking at migrating from a free account and want to grow your website. This might be the case if you are in the middle of reinventing yourself, or want to add ecommerce components. There might be other reasons, such as a business email.

Confession Time

Black Wolf Editorial Services (blackwolfeditorial.com) was hosted on WordPress.com for the first year of operation. I already had my author website there, and I knew how the system worked. So, I signed up for another free site and paid US$26 for the domain registration and privacy (at least, that's how much it was back then). I had set up an email alias, as I was entitled to do, so clients could contact me.

Then I got into a sticky situation where I couldn't respond to emails from the address that clients were using. I was forced to use another Gmail address. It looked incredibly unprofessional.

I elected to pay US$60 per year for a custom-domain Gmail account for the company. So, I had my single email address, a custom domain, and restrictions on what I could and couldn't do on my so-called *free* website that I was paying US$86 per year for.

Umm . . . Houston! We have a problem!

I couldn't believe I fell into the trap. This, folks, is how companies like WordPress actually make their money.

I did some investigative work, checking out reviews and talking to colleagues. For the same amount of money I was spending on the company site, I could have an unlimited number of emails and 100% control over my site. For a small amount extra, I could have all of my domains on the same server, each with their own unlimited number of emails.

In truth, if it wasn't for business-related decisions for my editorial company, I would likely still have my personal website with WordPress.com. But why should I spend more money than necessary for less flexibility?

I still use WordPress tools, but I'm now using WordPress.org tools, using a WordPress engine (similar to the WordPress.com sites) with added plugins to give me specific functionality.

There are a lot of different site-builder engines out there. WordPress just happens to be the most established and is highly portable between hosting providers.

If you are going to look at self-hosting for yourself, there are a few things to consider when looking at the various hosting providers.

THINGS TO CONSIDER

Let's assume that you are determined to have a self-hosted site, using the WordPress.org or some other page-building system. There are many steps involved.

Step One: Question your sanity.

Seriously. Web design can do your head in at the best of times. Granted, systems like WordPress.org make it relatively easy, but it can still cause you no end of headaches. If not handled with care, you could easily be left with a site that might look pretty but is unusable.

But let's assume the initial doubts of sanity have worn off, and you really do want to create a self-hosted site.

Step Two: Assess the different hosting providers.

I have lost count of the number of hosting providers out there, and what was good five years ago is not necessarily the best option today. Because of how fast the internet industry changes, I can't provide any recommendations for hosting providers.

If you are like me, you hate moving house—having to pack up the boxes and sort through the junk that you've accumulated over the years. So, choosing the right hosting provider is important, because you will likely be with them for years.

Get recommendations from your friends and colleagues. Find out who they use, and find out if they have had any negative experiences. Yes, you want to find out the *bad* here, because someone else's *bad* might be the smoking gun needed to help make a critical financial decision.

Check out the reviews from PC Magazine, PC World, or Macworld. (Yeah, those sites again. I did say that they would become your friends by the time we were done.)

And in this case, Google *is* your friend. Hunt out those negative reviews. Find out if these hosting providers really are what they say they are.

QUESTIONS TO ANSWER

There is a basic set of parameters to use when assessing hosting providers. It comes down to reliability and the ability to grow.

Here is a list of questions that you should be able to answer (even if you don't know what the numbers mean) before you pay the first bill.

1) How many websites are you allowed to host on a single plan?
2) How many email addresses can you have?
3) What type of hosting are you signing up for?
4) How much is it to transfer domain registration (assuming that you are coming from another hosting provider)?
5) What is the cost of privacy protection?
6) What sort of backup facilities are you provided with? What is the cost associated with this?
7) While you are getting a discount for your first contract, what are your renewal costs?
8) What type of SSL certificate are you given with your plan?
9) Which of the various page-builder tools are compatible with the servers?
10) How much disk space are you allocated?
11) What bandwidths do you get access to?
12) What sort of site downtime can you expect?

Some of these questions are self-explanatory, such as the number of websites (domains) you can have on a single plan, or the number of email addresses you're allowed to have. However, others can get bogged down with the technical details that tend to go over most people's heads.

Let's try to break this down so you know what this all means.

I apologize in advance, but I'm about to get technical. I'll do the best I can to keep the technobabble under control, but sometimes I can't help myself.

TYPES OF HOSTING

The most common type of hosting that people use is what is called *web hosting*, also called *shared hosting*. This is where multiple people have their data stored on the same remote server. Unless you are some big conglomerate company like Amazon, a *shared hosting* service will be more than sufficient. There really isn't the need for a *dedicated host server*.

You might encounter something called *cloud hosting*. This is for those wanting to do extensive computations in the background of their websites. Cloud hosting means that you can also share documents between various people within a company, creating your own cloud server like Dropbox. Again, this is unlikely to be something that the average writer is going to want to do with their website.

Then you have dedicated *WordPress hosting*. Be warned that this form of hosting is typically 10 to 20 times more expensive than your standard shared hosting for very little gain. But seeing this on offer (even if you don't want it) is a good thing. If the hosting company you're thinking about offers this, then you'll likely run into very few problems with using a WordPress installation on a shared-hosting site.

However, if you want to use WordPress tools, stay clear of those providers that make no mention whatsoever of WordPress within their advertising. You want a compatible server.

Domain Registration and Privacy

When you purchase a domain, you effectively rent it from another company who has registered it on your behalf. This registration process locks the domain to a particular host provider. However, anyone can look up who a site might be registered to.

If you go to whois.com, you can look up any domain and get a full rundown of who owns the site and who the administrator is. This is where privacy protection comes in.

For privately owned domains, the information retrieved in a WHOIS search will consist of when the domain was first registered, when it was last updated, when it comes up for renewal, and who the domain was registered through. But you will also have the contact details (i.e., postal address, email, and phone number) of the site owner (the registrant), the site administrator, and a technical contact for the site.

If you are using privacy protection (whatever it might be called), the contact details listed on the public record will belong to the company through which the domain was registered—not you. The site still belongs to you, but your contact details are hidden from the internet.

(By the way, WHOIS is not an acronym that stands for anything other than "who is". I never said that programmers were imaginative when naming things.)

Privacy protection will be an added charge to your domain hosting and registration, but it is worth the peace of mind. You really don't want your personal contact details (address and phone number) floating around the internet. Yes, your personal information can still be obtained by hackers, but at least the average John Doe won't have those details unless you choose to give them out.

Contact the company that you registered your domain through for more information about getting privacy protection.

Backups

We writers should back up our manuscripts on a regular basis, so why should our websites be any different? However, backing up a website is a complicated process.

It's more than just the pages and the pictures, but all the background coding to that website, too. It's the database entries that can't easily be replicated without a lot of hard work.

It is worth the money to have the service provider back up the site on a regular basis for you—only if you have a small quantity of data.

Your typical site, with hundreds of blog posts, images, and text, will be less than 1 GB (gigabyte). Most hosting services offer reasonably priced backup services for 1 GB of data.

For sites with a large number of videos and high-definition graphics, 1 GB will not be enough. As such, you will want to take the time to learn how to back up your own site. The cost of backing up sites larger than 1TB of data quickly becomes cost-prohibitive. Saying that, if your site is really that large, you might want to think about cleaning out old posts.

RENEWAL COSTS

This is something that's incredibly important to understand. Moving house can be a serious mission. So too can moving sites.

Host providers often offer cheap hosting at a fraction of their full price to entice new customers. If the renewal costs are outrageously high, then you have a problem. You don't want to keep moving if you don't have to.

The actual renewal costs should be clearly listed on the host provider's site.

SSL CERTIFICATES

SSL (Secure Socket Layers) are special protocols associated with the secure transfer of data across the internet. All websites today need an SSL certificate—even the free websites. A free *Google-friendly* SSL certificate gives your website the little padlock on the address bar within Chrome and other browsers. Without the SSL certificate, Chrome (and other website browsers) can refuse to open your website.

Because this is a known issue, reputable website hosting services (including the free ones) offer the Google-friendly SSL certificates for free.

However, if you are running an ecommerce site, selling your books or other products directly from your website, then you need an ecommerce SSL certificate. Sites like Shopify (a hosting provider dedicated to ecommerce sites) include the ecommerce SSL as part of their packages. Those running WordPress self-hosted websites will need to source their own ecommerce SSL certificates from their hosting providers.

Make sure you have the right SSL certificate for your website.

Page-builder Tools

There are so many page-builder tools out there. Some hosting providers have their own proprietary system, while others stick with the standard systems.

Providers like Shopify have their own systems, whereas SquareSpace and Hostgator allow you to use WordPress if desired.

WordPress is the most common page-builder system, and if you haven't gathered by now, it's the one I know the best. But even if you are running a WordPress site, you can install additional plugins to make your life easier.

I'm not going to dive into the different plugins in this book. Building websites is a book of its own. That said, you can find a list of useful plugins among the resources found at:

blackwolfeditorial.com/hidden-traps-book

Disk Space

Disk space is something that most computer users have a reasonable grasp of.

The larger the disk space available, the more data you can have on your website or included within your emails. Yes, you need to think about emails in this equation too.

When you contract a hosting provider to host your domain, you're also asking them to host your email server.

In today's society, you want to be using a server with IMAP protocols. IMAP gives you the ability to access your emails from any device (phone, tablet, computer email program, web, etc.) and know that you're seeing the same emails. Your sent emails are also backed up to the server under an IMAP protocol. Almost every company uses IMAP now. If they don't, stay away!

For a moment, let's talk about Google accounts. Yes, we're meant to be talking about self-hosted options, but this is the easiest way I can think of to explain the issues surrounding disk space.

Google provides 15 GB free of charge for its base accounts. This 15 GB is spread between your email, pictures stored on Google Photos, and files in your Google Drive. If you were to limit your Google account usage to just text-based information, 15 GB is a lot of data—it's a mountain of emails. However, the moment you add photos, music, or videos into that equation, 15 GB is gone before you know it.

Think about your phone. If you have a 32 GB SD card, how far does that get you before you have to start cleaning out old photos and files?

Web-hosting falls into the same category when it comes to disk space. Websites will have photos and possibly some videos too. Not everything will fall under the category of text. Emails will have attachments that can quickly fill up a mailbox.

Do not be skimpy with disk space, just because it was the cheaper option.

In an ideal world, your average page, with only text and no images, will take up approximately 50 KB. If you start adding lots of graphics to that, then your page could creep up to 1 MB. In some cases, it can be even more.

Say you have four static pages on your website, but have been blogging for years and have amassed in the order of 500 posts. Then your site is now 500 MB.

Now, let's say that you have videos on a quarter of your posts, and each video is in the order of 80 MB (not unreasonable for HD videos of 7 minutes in length). So, 125 posts that are 80 MB each . . . that's now at least 10 GB.

That plan that gave you 6 GB is now inadequate to service your needs. (There is a reason why many vloggers—those who have video blogs—use YouTube or Vimeo.)

BANDWIDTH

The amount of data that you are allowed to move around within a given month is presented to you as the *bandwidth*. It represents both download and upload traffic. This may be presented as so many MB per day or per month.

If your traffic is starting to approach your allocated limits, the load time of your site—the time it takes to load a single page in a web browser—will dramatically increase. What used to load in the blink of an eye might now take a few seconds to load. This is *not* a good thing.

Let's go back to our fictitious ideal site that is only 500 MB. Say you get 1,000 page views a day, equating to approximately 30,000 page views per month. (We can dream, right?) This means that your site would need a bandwidth allotment of 1.5 GB per month.

Most writers are never going to face bandwidth issues, but understanding what this actually means can help you gain a better appreciation for what your hosting provider is offering.

UPTIME AND DOWNTIME

Next, we come to something called *uptime*. Regardless of your views on bandwidth or disk space, it is vital that you understand how reliable your selected hosting provider is, and how often you can expect your servers to be out of action due to things like maintenance.

No hosting provider advertises 100% uptime. Sorry, guys, but they need to be able to maintain their systems, occasionally upgrading hardware and updating to the latest software. However, many providers advertise 99.99% uptime. What this means is that you can expect the servers to be down for a grand sum total of 53 minutes a year. This allows for regular scheduled maintenance and unexpected server outages.

Umm . . . perhaps it's just me, but 53 minutes throughout the year seems like a service that might as well be considered 24 hours a day, 7 days a week. Not really worth worrying about.

However, if your preferred hosting service provider is advertising 99% uptime, then you can expect your servers to be down 5,256 minutes per year, or 3.65 days. Now that's a number to be worried about. That provider might have some technical issues that could be problematic in the near future.

The situation is a little more complicated than you thought, huh?

In practice, most writers don't need to worry about these particular issues. If you are with a reputable self-hosting provider, you'll likely encounter few issues.

18

THE LOWDOWN ON WEB DESIGN

No two websites will have identical structures. Each website will have different elements, focusing on different aspects, because each person in charge of the various websites will have differing opinions on what is important.

When looking at the basics of web design, there are two aspects: the content and the look. As a writer, you may think that the content is the easy part. Don't be fooled.

There is a big difference between creating engaging stories that capture the imagination and writing clear web content that encourages a reader to check out the rest of your site. The skills might be similar, but the voice and tone are completely different.

For most websites, the look of your website will come down to the theme that you choose. There are thousands of themes to choose from, but they are all intended for different purposes. Some themes are well suited to photography, while others are better suited to small companies. Others will be intended for blogs about fitness and health, and others are best for blogs on film and TV.

When you choose a theme, there will be all the customization required to make the theme work for you: the colors, the sidebars, the menus, the social media icons, and so on.

After building nearly a dozen websites myself, consulting on half a dozen others, I understand why many writers are completely daunted by the task. There are so many things to think about. Far too often, the website is relegated to the *too-hard* basket.

Yes, you could hire a professional web designer to do it for you, but they will still require you to do the groundwork for them. You'll need to provide them with all the content and with a set of guidelines on how you want the site to look and feel. Even then, there is no guarantee that you'll have a site that you just love.

Here's a little secret: If you tell a web designer that you really don't know what you want, they will give you an off-the-shelf website with your content plugged into place and call it done. If you want that *unique* element, then you need to have an idea of what it is you actually want.

So, let's break down the basics of web design into components over the next several chapters.

19

CONTENT FOR A BASIC WEBSITE

HOPEFULLY, AT THIS POINT, I have already convinced you of the necessity of a website. No doubt, there are a few of you out there panicking about the idea, because it can seem like a big task. But your website doesn't need to be a complicated beast that is threatening to take over your writing time. In fact, a writer's website is incredibly simple if you strip away the shiny themes and the fancy widgets.

There is something to be said for the KISS method—Keep It Simple, Stupid—and in the realm of websites, the simpler, the better.

Any website needs to be built with a purpose in mind. This will dictate exactly what information is required on the static pages and how the pages should be structured.

An ecommerce site, designed so you can sell your books directly to your readers, will be structured differently than a simple author website that shares links to Amazon and other retailers for their books. A freelancer site, for say an editor or graphic designer, will be structured differently again. But there is core information that needs to be present on any author site.

A Basic Website

A website for a writer should include the following information at a minimum:

- information about the writer, detailing what you write, including genre and themes (an *About* page);
- a list of published works (if there are any), along with links on where those works can be found;
- a way in which to contact the writer (a *Contact* page or other links); and
- a privacy policy.

In today's internet world, the privacy policy is a legal requirement, and we will come back to this in chapter 23. But there is some other information that you will want to include too:

- your profile photos (normally included on your *About* page);
- links to key social media accounts (Facebook, Instagram, X, etc.)—but only include the accounts that are actively used;
- information about upcoming and ongoing projects; and
- a newsletter signup form—and make it easy to find.

If you have a blog, then you will likely have that on your website somewhere too. But please remember that a blog is *not* necessary to make it in this industry. Don't blog if you don't want to.

So . . . Ignoring the blog, the basic writer website is four pages: *About*, *Book*, *Contact*, and *Privacy Policy*. Links to your social media and newsletter signup forms will be peppered around the site, likely in the footers or on the sidebars (if your theme includes footers and sidebars).

There is no need to make it any more complicated than that—unless you want to.

ADDITIONAL USEFUL PAGES

If you are a bit further down the path of your writing career, a basic four-page website might not be enough. There are a couple of additional pages and some additional content that you will want to add.

An established writer's website might include the following:

- a backlist catalog that includes all of your published works, including the historic out-of-print stuff;
- individual book pages for in-print books;
- extensive contact information, which might include your agent or publicist; and
- a press kit, complete with downloadable photos. (I recommend new writers have a press kit too, which is why you'll find full details for press kits in chapter 24.)

You might even incorporate a special landing page that highlights your latest publication.

Even with the additional information, it's still a simple website, with a small number of pages, depending on the number of books you have published.

A BASIC FREELANCER'S WEBSITE

Many writers are freelance service providers on the side. I am. While the websites are similar, the core information required is different, simply because the purpose of the site is different.

I know some freelancers choose to host the information about their services on their writer websites. I have mixed feelings about this, because the purpose of a writer website is completely different to that of a freelancer website. The audiences are different.

On a writer website, you are trying to showcase your writer self and the works that you want people to read. But a freelancer website is not about you. It's about the services you provide and how you can help your clients.

Ultimately, the decision is up to you, but I would consider separate sites for marketing reasons.

But let's look at how the basic website changes for a freelancer site.

Well, the *About* page becomes information about how you can help your clients and what they can expect if they hire you.

The *Book* page disappears, because you won't include a list of published works, unless those published works are in direct service to your clients. However, you might include a *Testimonial* page or a *Portfolio* of work that you have done for clients.

I always enjoy looking at the covers that graphic designers have done. It really showcases their abilities. And it's fun to look at the list of books that an editor has edited (assuming that their clients have gone on to publish those books).

Your *Contact* page will possibly become a *contact form* for client onboarding, where you seek basic information about a client's project as part of your initial onboarding process.

You are still legally required to include a *privacy policy*, and you will still want to build an email list and share your social media links.

But a freelancer website is just as simple a beast as the writer website.

Let's take a deeper look at each of the four core pages in the next few chapters.

20
THE ABOUT PAGE

THE *ABOUT* PAGE ON a website serves one purpose: to give the reader information about who you are, what you do, and why you do it. As such, your bio will be the most important component of an *About* page. However, you might also include a profile photo and some basic contact information.

THE BIO

Back in chapter 13, we went into detail about writing bios, but as a reminder, your bio needs to be able to answer the following questions.

1) What genre do you write?
2) What drives you to do what you do?
3) What are some of your accomplishments?
4) What else do you do?

While bios are typically written in third person, on your *About* page specifically, you might want to write it in first person. Do what feels right to you.

This particular variant of your bio will most likely only ever appear on your website. There is no need to turn it into an essay of its own.

The bio on your *About* page shouldn't be any longer than one or two scrolls of the page. Anything longer than that is unlikely to be read, except by the die-hard fans.

Your Experience

If your website is for a freelancer or company, your *About* page is your chance to tell people why they should trust you with their time and money.

As a reminder, a bio for a service provider should be able to answer the following questions.

1) What experience do you have highlighting that you understand your clients' needs?
2) What benefits will your client get if they work with you?
3) What steps are involved in starting that process?
4) What sort of experience can they expect working with you?

While none of the questions above talk about qualifications, on your *About* page, you might want to include a list of your qualifications and professional memberships or affiliations. But include it *after* your bio, as that extra carrot for those who aren't totally convinced by your bio on its own.

Go back to chapter 13 for more details on writing a bio for a service provider.

Profile Photo

Your *About* page will also include a photo of yourself of some kind. For a writer, this will likely be a photo of yourself that shows you in the best light possible. It could be a photo of you cuddling your dog, or living your life in the woods near home. Whatever photo you choose, ensure that it's reflective of your personality. (Go back to chapter 12 for more details on profile photos.)

For a company, it's common to see a photo of the office buildings on the *About* page. For those who run businesses from home, you might want to use the same image that you would if it was a personal site.

CALL-TO-ACTION

Your *About* page should also contain a call-to-action in addition to your bio and profile image.

Call-to-actions are the sentences and phrases that suggest that readers follow you on X, or like your Facebook page, or sign up for your newsletter. Call-to-action links are a form of subliminal marketing.

Websites and blogs should contain call-to-action links somewhere on almost every post and page. These could be "*get a sample of my latest book here*", at which point you've sent your reader to Amazon, Kobo Books, or wherever. Just as long as those calls-to-action links can be found somewhere.

21
Contact Page

The *Contact* page provides visitors to your site with a way to contact you.

It is a legal requirement to have valid contact information on your website, *not* just links to your social media. Some countries require that you include a postal address on your website, too. (I know Australia requires this.) But exactly how much detail you provide, other than what is legally required, is up to you.

Businesses often include phone numbers, postal addresses, and customer inquiry emails.

As an individual, I would advise against phone numbers unless you are legally required to include a phone number in your country. And for postal addresses, I would advise using a PO Box or virtual office address. Try to avoid listing your home address. (It's a security thing. Delusions of grandeur . . . and stalkers are real!)

Contact Forms

For writers and businesses alike, I highly recommend the use of contact forms. These can be as simplistic or complicated as you like. However, the more complicated something is, the less likely someone is to use it.

At a minimum, you should collect the name of the person contacting you, an email address, and a comment or message. You might also want to include a website or other related details.

Personally, I don't bother with a subject field, as I'm able to specify a unique marker within my form design.

Most contact forms allow you to specify the email address that entries go to, and it doesn't need to be you—it could be an assistant. For that matter, you can have those entries going to multiple email addresses.

Contact forms also use reCAPTCHA fields, weeding out the bots. With reCAPTCHA on your forms, you know that all users are human, but that doesn't mean they're genuine. You will still need to manually filter incoming emails to a certain extent. For more information on reCAPTCHA, visit:

google.com/recaptcha/about

> Do not link your contact form to your newsletter list.

This practice will land you in hot water faster than you can take your clothes off to jump into the bath. Even if you make it clear that using the form will add them to your email list, connecting those contact forms to your email list is unethical. Keep the signup forms for your newsletter separate from your general contact form.

Even if you include a contact form, it is advisable that you also share a communications email within the text of the page. But remember that bots will scrape your website for email addresses, and will send you spam and scams. As such, use a *public-facing communications email* for this. (Go back to chapter 4 for more information about the different types of emails a writer needs.)

POSSIBLE ADDITIONAL INFORMATION

The *Contact* page should include all contact information for your various projects. If you are traditionally published, include the contact details for your agent (if you have one). If you have a publicist, include their information here too.

In general, if there is another person who manages a particular aspect of your writing career, include their details on your *Contact* page. If no other details are present, then all communication will come directly to you.

22

BOOK PAGES

THE PUBLICATIONS SECTION OF your website will be a dynamic beast that will grow, becoming multiple pages, as you write more and publish more. Exactly how these pages are laid out will depend on a variety of factors, including your site's theme.

A quick side note for those still working on their first publications: Don't feel pressured to publish something right away. Take your time to edit and polish that story to the best of your ability.

The *Book Pages* is one aspect of your website that you can take the time to build. Do it when you are ready.

To help keep this simple, let's look at the individual books first.

SINGLE BOOK LISTING

I'm of the school of thought that every book should have its own dedicated page on your website. However, this is not necessary. Regardless, for each book, you will want to include a cover image, a brief blurb, and buy links at a minimum.

For those using separate pages for each book, you might want to include a sample (or links to samples), reviews, ISBNs (or ASINs for Amazon-only publications), and any other information that might be useful.

Ensure that your blurb is the same as that listed on your back cover or on your store listings. I recommend that cover images be restricted to no bigger than 300 pixels in width to help speed up your website's load speed. (Larger images might be required on other sites, but this restriction is just for your site. We want those pages to load as fast as possible.)

Include the buy links to as many places as possible where readers can get your book. Hopefully, you have affiliate links for the various stores, so you can earn a little extra cash from each sale.

The Main Publications Page

Your main publications page will be a collective look at everything that you have published. The exact structure of this page will depend entirely on your body of work.

If you have multiple series, you might showcase the first book in each of the series, then have a *series* page for each series. If this is the case, ensure that you list the order that each book appears in the series, especially if reading those books out of order will have a negative impact on the reader experience.

Include any upcoming publications available for preorder. Showcase your back catalog. Even include any out-of-print books, so your readers can see your full body of work.

For multiple publications, a table layout of book covers works well, where each book cover links to their respective individual book pages.

Irrespective of the layout you ultimately use, keep your main publications page as simple as possible.

MyBookTable Plugin for WordPress

If you are using a self-hosted WordPress website, consider using the *MyBookTable* plugin from Stormhill Media. It is free to use, and you can install it directly from the plugin menu within the backend of your website. Majority of the features you would want to use are integrated as part of the *free* plan, including Amazon Affiliate integration.

I use this plugin on all of the sites that I administer, because it makes it easy to quickly load a book into the system. The plugin generates all the pretty pages and the interlinking between the pages, including if you have a book in a series. If you add the ASIN number from Amazon into the backend, you even get those pretty preview pages showing up directly on your site. No need to visit Amazon, except perhaps to buy the book.

I have a paid subscription to this plugin, which also generates the pretty grid layouts to showcase a large number of books. To see this plugin in action, check out my recommended books list on Black Wolf Editorial Services found at:

blackwolfeditorial.com/resources/books

I do not get anything out of recommending the *MyBookTable* plugin to others, except the joy in seeing authors create awesome book pages on their websites—quickly!

PUBLICATIONS THAT ARE NOT BOOKS

Not all publications will be books. Some might be guest blog posts. Or maybe you have short stories or personal essays published in anthologies or magazines.

For anything published in a magazine or anthology, I would treat it like a book. Use the cover of the magazine or anthology, and list the *buy links* for the larger body of work.

For guest blog posts, my inclination would be to compile a list of your guest blog posts onto one page. For each guest spot, give it a linked title (linking to the article on the external site) and a teaser that describes what the post was about. Include information about when it was posted and on what site. I would also include a *Read Post* link at the bottom of the listing, so your site visitors don't need to scroll up for the link.

List your most recent guest blog posts at the top of the page. This will serve two purposes.

1) It will ensure that visitors to the page see your latest blog post listings without having to scroll to see them. (This is why blog feeds always include the latest post at the top of the list.)

2) It simplifies the maintenance process of your guest blog posts page. After a certain date (where blog posts are of a certain age), you can remove those listings. Because those listings are at the bottom of the page, you don't have to do anything fancy to clean up the formatting of the page itself.

An additional maintenance tip: For any guest blog posts no longer available on the external site, either remove the listing or update the listing to state that the post is no longer externally available. And consider posting that no-longer-available post on your own blog, assuming you have a blog and assuming that the post fits within the theme of your blog.

If you would like to take a look at how I manage guest blog posts on my own site, visit:

judylmohr.com/about/publications/guest-blog-posts

23

THE PRIVACY POLICY

IF YOU ARE NEW to the idea of websites, you are likely wondering if you really need to have a privacy policy.

The simple answer: Yes.

The more complicated answer: You legally don't have a choice.

If you have a website, you are collecting personal data. Because of international privacy laws, any user of the internet is entitled to know exactly what it is that you do with the personal data you collect. With privacy practices being legally challenged in a big way in recent times, it's more important than ever before to ensure your readers know exactly how their data is being used.

I can hear someone complaining, saying that they aren't collecting personal data (probably someone who doesn't have an email list). But trust me, just by having a website, you are collecting personal data.

If you have a contact form on your website, you are collecting personal data. If you have a newsletter subscription form on your website, you're collecting personal data. If you provide your email address (or phone number) and encourage readers to contact you that way, you're collecting personal data. And every time anyone visits a page on your website, you're collecting IP addresses that tell you from where in the world someone accessed your website.

It doesn't matter if you have no idea what to actually do with that information, you're still collecting it.

Most websites today use what is known as *cookies*. These are little data packets that help a website to track a user's activities on a site. These cookies might seem harmless, allowing users to remain logged in to their favorite social media sites (Facebook, X, Instagram, etc.), but some cookies will also return MAC addresses to the website's server. The MAC address is a specific code that relates to the motherboard on your device. This is how systems like Dropbox, Google Drive, and OneDrive know exactly when, and if, another device is connected to your account, and how they are able to give you the ability to *log out on all devices* through the web.

Even if the cookies used on your website are not that sophisticated, you are still collecting personal data.

Now, to totally do your head in.

If you have a social media account and you are interacting with others on those sites (which you should be doing with social media), you are collecting personal data.

Everything we do on the web results in the transfer of personal data. And if your interactions are in a business-related context (and being a writer is like being a small business owner), then you are legally required to inform people how you use their personal data.

There is no getting around this. You don't want to be the one writer who faces court action because of a breach of privacy.

To cover your ass, just have a privacy policy and move on.

Let's be realistic here. How many people sign up to a service and hit the *"I Agree"* button without reading the Terms of Use or Privacy Policy? (ME! ME! I'll raise my hand, because I'm probably one of the guiltiest people out there for this one. I could be agreeing to sell my firstborn and not know it. But if anyone really wants to pay for the food he eats, by all means, take him.)

Your privacy policy doesn't need to be anything fancy. In fact, it doesn't even need to be serious. When I wrote the privacy policy for my personal website, I chose to have fun and be snarky as hell. It's 100% me. More on that below.

Clauses Needed at a Minimum

> Quick Disclaimer: I'm not a lawyer, so you can't call this legal advice by any stretch of the definition. I'm just sharing the information and knowledge that I've amassed along the way.

There are some core clauses that you should include in your privacy policy. Whether you are snarky or serious, you need to mention the following.

Who are you? Who are people granting permission to?

Phrase I use:

> *I'm a writer and seriously underpaid freelance editor, working my knuckles to the bone to break even here.*

What data is collected?

Phrase I use:

> *You're visiting my website, so the system knows where you are. Just accept it, okay? I use Google Analytics, primarily to stare at pretty little graphs of real-time stats, because who doesn't like pretty graphs.*

Another phrase I use:

> *I also have a contact form, because how else are you meant to contact me? I suppose you could use social media, but contact forms are more funky.*

How is the data used?

Phase I use:

> *I don't sign you up for my newsletter unless you click the link that says "Subscribe" in one of its many variations. In which case, your name and email address fly through the internet to MailerLite, which is the system I use to manage my newsletters and email lists.*

Who has access to your systems?

Phrase I use:

> *When I say I, I really mean me, a lowly writer and freelance editor, seriously underpaid, and the ~~slaves~~ volunteers who pick up the slack when my computer blows up and has a complete meltdown.*

Reminder that people can disable cookies.

Phrase I use:

> *If you don't want the delicious home-baked scripts that come with WordPress (or the internet as a whole), you can block them through your browser, but don't come crying to me when nothing works and you can't see anything on my website.*

Reminder of right to be forgotten.

Phrase I use:

Yeah, I use email. Yes, I have an email address book. No, you can't see my address book, because it's my address book. In fact, the only reason you would ever be in my address book is if you sent me an email first, or used my contact form. However, if you want me to delete your email from my address book, sure . . . Consider it done.

Another Phrase I use:

Sure. Whatever. If you insist. If you are really that scared of me, then contact me and tell me to f*** off, and I'll delete all the little packets of information that I can find on you from my system. Then I'll likely turn you into a dead body in one of my manuscripts, changing your name so you never know the truth . . . but I'll know.

How is data stored?

Phrase I use:

I'm a data junky, keeping backups on external hard drive, and within the cloud. (Yes, I use the cloud.) I'm obsessed with backing up data, BECAUSE MY COMPUTER HATES ME!

What will happen in the event of a security breach?

Phrase I use:

> *In the event of a data breach, I will let you know in a timely manner and take full responsibility. For example, the cat might decide that he's had enough of lying in the window behind my monitor and for a brief moment saunters past the keyboard (walking on it as he does), I will pick him up and tell him off in a big way. He's not supposed to be on my desk, anyway.*

I did mention that your privacy policy doesn't need to be serious, right? As a writer, make sure that every page on your website, including your privacy policy, is a reflection of who you are. And if you haven't worked out that I'm one snarky bugger, I have failed as a writer.

If you want to have a peek at my full privacy policy, visit:

judylmohr.com/about/privacy-policy

But if you want to be *serious* with your privacy policy—maybe your brand doesn't lend itself to being a smart-ass like me—then run a Google search for "generate privacy policy". The number of free privacy policy generators that pop up is insane. Just pick one and use it . . . after you've tailored it to fit your branding, of course.

Take a look at the privacy policies of your favorite authors. That said, it's alarming how many authors still don't have privacy policies on their websites. They don't see it as important . . . but peeps, to be *legal*, it is required!

24
THE PRESS KIT

SOME YEARS AGO, I encountered a blog post that spoke about the importance of having a press kit on your website, even if you were a debut writer. By a press kit, they meant having downloadable pictures and copies of your bio in various formats, and of course, information about your new book. The press kit could be used by anyone for almost any purpose, but it was a form of advertising.

I have no idea on what blog I saw that post, but I remember getting my A into G and putting together a press kit page for my personal website, complete with information about the book that was being released at the time. Since then, I have updated the page to focus on more recent publications, and I keep updating it.

In 2019, I discovered just how important press kit pages are.

In preparation for the 2019 Romance Writers New Zealand (RWNZ) Conference, I was tasked with getting the programs and other bits of printing sorted. Well . . . When I got the files, the program contained profile images of all the speakers, logos of the businesses taking part in the trade show, and sponsor logos. About half of the profile photos for the guest speakers were grainy. I needed to source *new* profile images, because the resolution within the original files was insufficient for printing.

Could I *find* decent print-ready images on the various author websites? You have got to be kidding me! In one case (for a keynote speaker no less), the only profile photo on her website was 150 x 100 pixels. Sure, it looked great online, making it easy to load on a cellphone, but there was *no way* that I could use that image for printing.

And hence, the importance of a press kit, regardless of where you are at within your writing career.

Writers, please create a press kit page. This is not your *About* page, but rather a separate page on your site where people can go to download print-ready (and web-ready) versions of your profile photo, get a bio that they can copy and paste onto their site (complete with links), information about your latest publications (if you have any) and any other downloadables that are used for promotional purposes. This includes the cover images of your latest books, if appropriate, or press releases about upcoming book tours and other projects.

It's not hard to put together. You need all that information for yourself, anyway. Just compile it into one location, so people don't have to hunt around on your website to find the information they need. Make it easy for them. Make it easy on yourself.

Back in May 2019, I presented at the New Zealand Society of Authors (NZSA) Canterbury Writers workshops. When I was asked for a profile photo, I sent the link to my press kit page to the coordinator and invited them to download whatever image they needed. It kept the email size down, because I wasn't sending a giant print-ready image that was over 3 MB through email. (I've been known to have print-ready promo images on my press page that are 6 MB. Imagine sending that through email. Ugh!) And if they wanted a different image than the one I would have sent, they had their choice of at least two others.

Any time someone asks me for a bio (for any purpose), guess where I go to get it.

Seriously, peeps, have a press kit page. It makes life easier.

WHAT TO INCLUDE ON A PRESS KIT PAGE

The list below is what I have on my press kit page. I have bolded the items that I feel are the bare minimum for a press kit page.

Standard profile image
- **Web-ready version shown**
- **Link to web-ready download**
- **Link to print-ready download**

Alternative profile image (close-up image)
- Web-ready version shown
- Link to web-ready download
- Link to print-ready download

Micro-bio (single sentence tag line)

Short bio (single paragraph)

Long bio (full bio used for introductions)

Social Media links
- **Active profiles only**
- Published authors include Amazon and Goodreads too

Latest Book Information
- **Image of cover**
- Link to web-ready downloadable image
- **Blurb about the book**
- **Links to where the book can be purchased**
- If it's not out yet, include the release date.

Other books you want to promote
- Include cover, blurb, buy links, and images

Additional promotional images
- Web-ready version shown
- Link to web-ready download
- Link to print-ready download

Depending on what stage you are at in your career, you might also want to include links to recent interviews and other tidbits of information.

Print-ready and Web-ready Image Resolution

When we talk about print-ready or web-ready images, we're talking about the number of pixels in the image file. The more pixels compacted into a tiny space, the higher resolution. Seems simple enough, yet people still get it wrong.

Let me try to put some numbers to this issue in a way that everyone can understand.

I run two 24-inch wide-screen monitors for my computer. The physical dimensions of my main monitor is 21 inches wide (54 cm) by 12 inches tall (30 cm). (For those who don't know, monitors and TV screens are advertised using the diagonal measurement, which is 24 inches.) I use a resolution of 1920 x 1080 pixels, which is the recommended resolution for my monitors. This means, that my monitors use a resolution of 90 dpi (dots per inch).

This resolution is standard for monitors and other electronic devices. However, for high-quality printing, you *need* 300 dpi, at a minimum.

Remember how I said above that I encountered one author's profile image that was approximately 150 x 100 pixels. Well, on my screen, that image would render as 1.6 x 1.1 inches, assuming that the website was not employing any image scaling (and for those who know anything about basic HTML coding, there is normally some sort of image scaling employed on websites). If I was to take that exact same image and configure it for high-resolution printing, then it would print at 0.5 x 0.3 inches. That's dinky! You might think that you can just scale up that image to the respectable 3 x 2 inches, but all you get is a pixelated mess, certainly not the professional printed image.

Enter the growling monster that is asked to print that disaster and make it look good. Grr!

On a website, *any* website, you should be using profile images that are at least 300 x 300 pixels. Ideally, you should be using something that is 500 pixels in its shortest dimension.

In 2023, Facebook recommended 196 x 196 pixels for your profile images as a minimum. However, on a computer they would display those images as 176 x 176 pixels on your main profile, rendered on my monitor as just shy of 2 inches across. Remember my monitor uses 90 dpi, so that 2-inch image is using 180 pixels.

Do you see where I'm going here?

For close-up profile images, ensure that your web-ready image can be truncated to a *300 x 300 pixel square* centered around your face and still renders appropriately on your computer screen. The print-ready version needs to be triple this in size, i.e., *900 x 900 pixel square* centered around your face.

The pixel sizes listed above are the minimum requirements.

BIOS

I'm not going to go into the full detail about how to write a micro, short, or long bio. I covered that back in chapter 13. All I can say is that it makes your life so much easier if you already have these written, particularly the *short bio*.

I've lost count of the number of times I've been asked for a short bio, one paragraph in length. Where do you think I go to get it?

Some variant of my short bio is used on almost every site where I have participated in guest blogs, interviews, or presenting. Even my Amazon and Goodreads pages contain some variant of my short bio.

Are you starting to see the usefulness of the press kit page?

BOOKS AND PUBLICATIONS

Sure, you'll have book information on other pages too, especially if you have a decent-sized book list. On your press kit page, you will include only the information about your latest book and any other publications that you are currently promoting.

Make it easy for book promoters to get everything they need to help you promote your book. That includes the cover image, a blurb, and links to where one can buy the book.

If you have a self-hosted WordPress site, seriously consider using the *MyBookTable* plugin by Stormhill Media. All book pages on my websites have been created by using this plugin.

What I like most about this plugin is the ability to easily include information about the book I'm promoting wherever I want on my website. I tell the shortcode generator which book I want the information for, and the plugin pulls the information needed from the individual book page and shows it on my press kit page (or any other page where I want the information shown). So many hours saved by this plugin.

STILL WORKING TOWARDS PUBLICATION?

If you don't have any publications, that's okay. Don't panic! They will come. You could still put together the other aspects of your press kit page.

SOCIAL MEDIA LINKS

Even if you advertise your social media links elsewhere on your site, make sure that they are easy to find on your press kit page too. Social media forms a huge part of an author's online platform. Don't overlook it!

Include your Goodreads author page and your Amazon author page in your list of social media too (if you have them).

FINAL THOUGHTS ON PRESS KIT PAGES

The press kit page is a tool used for marketing purposes. Put anything that you want out there as marketing on that page.

It is so easy to overlook the importance of such a page, but as I mentioned at the start of this chapter, I got decidedly grumpy because I wasn't able to find the images I needed to create a printable version of the 2019 RWNZ Conference program. I was able to get what I needed in the end, but I have the knowledge, the technical know-how, and the software to create high-resolution photos out of web-ready resolution images (assuming that they were more than 150 x 100 pixels). I know what I'm doing, which is part of the reason the conference coordinator asked me to deal with that part of the program.

However, I'm a rare breed of internet user. Most people just use the information they're given and don't think about image quality. It's not their problem if something looks poor because the author couldn't be bothered to give them something suitable.

Having a press kit page, with web-ready and print-ready images, deals with all those issues and more.

If you would like to look at my press kit page, visit:

judylmohr.com/about/press-kit

25

Look and Feel
It's More than a Theme

The content of a website, while vitally important, is only part of the equation. That information needs to be presented in a way that it entices people to keep reading. If you do anything that visitors to your site find annoying, you will have lost a potential reader.

However, you are not going to make everyone happy. There will always be those who find something to nit-pick about. If you try to create the perfect website, you'll go insane.

You want a website that works for you, taking advantage of the current technology and web design philosophies. But even the digital marketing experts get things wrong. They make suggestions based on the latest trend, but sometimes those trends infuriate people and aren't suited to the publishing industry.

Whether you go through the nightmare efforts of designing your own website or hire a web designer to do it for you, there is one rule that I would highly recommend you stick to. If you find a particular feature or design element annoying and ugly to look at, assume your readers will too. It doesn't matter what the experts say: don't allow anything on your site that would infuriate you.

Web design is about the end-user experience. Fancy headers and scrolling pages are all well and dandy, but if they fail to leave a positive impact, you might as well not have a website at all.

Even if you decide to fork out the big bucks on a web designer, you will need a rudimentary understanding of web design basics, just so you can describe the look and feel that you're after.

As I mentioned before, gone are the days of needing to code each individual page for a website. Today, everything is based on themes, providing the ability to quickly change the look and feel of any website with a few clicks of a mouse. There are thousands of themes that one could choose from, and more seem to come out every day.

When trying to decide how your own website should look and function, do a little surfing and find a few sites that you like the look and feel of. Make notes of any common features. If possible, see if you can identify the theme used; some sites will include theme information in the footer. On your little surfing journey, make notes of features that frustrate you. These are the features that you want to avoid.

Look at the color schemes used. Some themes allow users to change individual elements, while others will have predefined color scheme options. Keep in mind that colors on a site are not necessarily the only colors available.

Take note of how individual posts behave with respect to the main blog feed. Individual blog posts often employ a different header and sidebar structure to the rest of the site. In some cases, a blog post might have a feature image that isn't visible on the individual post, but only seen on the main blog feed page. If you carefully chose that feature image, this trait might be undesirable.

Pay attention to fonts and font sizes. Do you need to zoom in to see the text? Is the text so big that it takes an insane number of scrolls to get to the bottom of the page?

Are you losing your mind yet?

Let's take a step back and talk about some of the features of a website that are highly desirable . . . or could catch you unaware. Time to define some terms common to the web design world.

THE HOME PAGE

A *home page* is the page that a person is directed to when they type in your domain name. The home page might be a static page or your main blog feed (assuming you have a blog).

The static variant might contain information about your latest release, or it could contain a menu of sorts that leads visitors to other portions of your site. If you go with the static page option and you have a blog on your site, then you will need to create a page for your blog feed.

There are no right or wrong options with this one. Do what you feel works best.

Don't confuse a home page with a *landing page*. While a home page *is* a landing page, it won't be the only landing page on your website. A landing page is any page where a visitor enters the site. If you have a blog, then each blog post will be a landing page too.

SIDEBARS, HEADERS, AND FOOTERS

Headers for websites come in all shapes and sizes.

Some will include the name of the site and a menu bar. Other sites will put the name of the site and menu bar on a sidebar, employing no header for a desktop version of the site.

Some themes have placeholders for logos. The place for this is typically in the header of the site, commonly on the left-hand side or center of the screen. As a writer, you might not have a logo (I don't), but that's okay. The themes that accommodate logos typically permit you to use formatted words instead.

Whether you have a logo or not, it is vital that you include the name of the site in any header, so that it will appear on every page and post.

There is a school of thought that one should use pages without headers. For a main site page, this is just crazy talk. Visitors to your site need to know they are on the right site.

Sidebars have become popular among websites for use on desktop browsers. Sites like Facebook have two sidebars, one on either side of the screen. However, the number of sidebars you choose to employ for your website will depend on personal preference and your selected theme.

Many sites also include footers, but not all. If you use a footer, ensure that you include a basic copyright statement. Also, include call-to-action links, such as links to your external social media, subscription to your mailing list, or links to other pages that you would like people to visit.

WIDGETS

Widgets provide added functionality to a website design in a self-contained box that is often configured separately. They are often seen as small sub-windows on the sidebars, headers, or footers.

A widget might be used for your newsletter subscription form. Or maybe you showcase the posts from your favored social media directly on your website. Widgets could contain fancy buttons that link to your social media, a recent-post selector, etc. In some cases, a widget might contain a special sub-menu of carefully curated pages.

Be selective of the widgets you use. You do not want to employ so many widgets down your sidebars that your sidebars are significantly longer than the standard length of posts or pages.

As a general rule of thumb, if it takes more than two or three scrolls of the mouse to get to the bottom of the sidebars, then you are likely using too many widgets.

Responsive Layouts

Using a smartphone or tablet to read emails and blog posts is now common practice. As such, website designs need to accommodate these smaller screens without turning into mouse print.

Modern websites employ *responsive* themes. These themes rearrange the site elements to make them more legible on the screen viewing them. These themes even respond to a reader flipping a tablet between portrait to landscape mode.

As an added incentive to use a responsive theme, Google penalizes sites that don't have a mobile-friendly format, decreasing a site's SEO ranking.

You do not need to pay a fortune for these themes. For years, I have used Vantage from SiteOrigin for my self-hosted WordPress sites, and it's free.

Just a word of advice: When setting up a new website theme, even if you're familiar with the overall components, view your site on multiple devices with different browsers. Make sure that the responsive nature of your theme layout is behaving in expected ways.

Check how your pages appear on all devices and for various screen widths. What looks good on your 17-inch monitor at full screen may look cramped when viewed on a smaller window. On a mobile device, menus are often condensed to the three-line symbol. If you employ a complex menu structure, your readers may struggle to navigate your site.

Placement of images within text needs to be such that text doesn't become a thin, narrow strip of single words when viewed on narrow screens. If need be, put images centered on the page with no text around them.

Be mindful of the number of widgets in your sidebars and footers. For narrow screens, widgets on a responsive layout appear under the main text. However, some themes will put the widgets from the headers before the text. You don't want your main text obscured and bogged down by widgets.

COLOR CONTRAST AND WHITE SPACE

The concept of *white space* originates from old-school printing. To make a page easier to read, the paragraph formatting needed to be handled in such a way that there was a sufficient amount of blank space surrounding the text, breaking it up. But when considering the blank space around the text (the white space), you are also looking at the margins, any paragraphing indentations or gaps between paragraphs, gaps around images, and the sizes of headers.

The term white space does not mean that your blank areas need to be *white*. On a screen, particularly a back-lit screen, a bright white background can be harsh on the eyes. Many apps that you can get on your phone have recognized this issue and now provide users with the ability to change to a *night mode* setting. And for most devices, *night mode* means white text on a black (or near black) background.

Many web designers deliberately take action to change the colors of a site to move away from the harsh white. They preserve the concept of white space by ensuring that there is plenty of blank space surrounding the text and images.

In an attempt to remove the harsh white/black contrast entirely from a site, it has become common for sites to use gray text, i.e., a light gray on a black background or a dark gray on a white background. It is a good idea to play around with these gray levels. However, be careful. There is a point when the use of gray removes the contrast needed to make the text legible.

Never put dark text on a dark background. Never put light text on a light background. If you want people to read your website, there needs to be a contrast in the colors used.

This concept of contrast is something that designers of retail sites have gotten a firm grasp of. Buttons on Amazon are a yellow-orange, making them stand out when placed against the blue and black text.

Some conversion-rate specialists recommend using green and red buttons. However, if you do use green and red on your site, you need to take red/green color blindness into consideration. It's surprisingly common, occurring in approximately 8% of the male population. If you were to place two buttons side by side, one red and one green, a site visitor might not be able to make the distinction between the two buttons.

Popups

Popups are those forms that suddenly appear on the screen, demanding that you take whatever action they want you to take before you can proceed to read the page.

I can't think of anyone that I know who likes popups. They are typically seen as obtrusive and annoying. While they still seem to be the favored way to boost newsletter signups, there is a major downside to using popups (besides irritating people).

Google penalizes sites that use automatic popups on mobile devices. This means that unless you can specify that your popup shows only on desktop browsers, using that popup could hurt you.

Pages Without Menus

This is a common trend among content marketers: using landing pages without menus, or any other method of getting off the page and onto the main site, other than performing the action that the site owner wants you to perform (often to buy something). And even the purchase doesn't necessarily take you back to the website.

Many online courses operate like this, and I'll admit that I have mixed feelings about this tactic. I often find myself scrolling right to the bottom of the page, trying to find the one bit of information that I actually want: the price. And most of the time, I just close the window and walk away. The mountain of scrolling often turns me off before I get to the price tag.

If you are going to use a page without menus for marketing reasons, make sure that the page is short.

Those pages without menus have one purpose and one purpose only: sales. You are trying to convince the visitor to give you something (money or their email) in exchange for something in return. Don't hold the information about the price until the bottom. Put it up front.

Don't be the pushy salesman, trying to flob off the lemon, who refuses to drop the other shoe.

ADS AND MONETIZATION

A good number of writers monetize their websites by adding ads via Google AdSense or some other affiliate's program. These programs generate money for the site just because someone visits a page with a given ad.

There are many people out there who say they hate the intrusive nature of ads. However, I'm guessing that the site owners haven't configured, or have poorly configured, the ads that appear on their sites.

With Google AdSense, you can specify which pages ads appear on, how big the ads are, and where on the page they are shown. You can also restrict and block certain categories of ads, or a specific ad, from your site.

I don't use Google ads on my own sites, but I do have affiliate links connected to the books that I recommend.

Programs like the Amazon Affiliates provide you with unique link codes to products available on the site's store. If someone purchases the item using the link you provided them, you collect a small commission. These are different from ads in the conventional sense in that they are just links. If you are advertising your own books, you collect a royalty plus a commission because a reader used your link.

There are other ways to monetize your sites too, but treat all programs with care. Don't become that pushy used-car salesman.

FORGOTTEN SETTINGS

There are other settings for a site that can sometimes be neglected.

Ensure that the site title and tagline are set from within the site's settings. Also set an icon image. The icon image and your site title are what appears in the title bar of a browser window when someone visits your website. But that tagline (if not used by your site's theme) gets picked up by the SEO algorithms. And all three will sometimes show in the search results on Google and Bing.

Change the site's time zone to your local time zone. It's frustrating to set a publication date for a blog post, only to discover that it didn't go live when you expected it to.

If your site uses comments and discussions, ensure that all new comments are moderated manually. You can elect to have comments from previously approved posters accepted automatically, but you don't want your comments to be taken over by those annoying bots which are advertising random things. Be advised that if any commenter becomes annoying (a troll in the making), you can have their email added to a blacklist, denying them access to *submit-comment* features on your site.

And for those of you with self-hosted sites, remember to update your plugins on a regular basis too. Those updates will contain additional features and security updates that will help to protect your website.

GET ANOTHER SET OF EYES

Just like writing, where it is imperative that you gain feedback from others, I strongly recommend that you do the same for a website. You may have chosen colors or fonts that you adore, but others might find the combination obtrusive and jarring.

It is also important to have another person check links and other features that you might have on your website. You could have a mountain of broken links, or your contact form might be going to an email address that doesn't exist.

Your site-tester buddies do not need to have a background in web design. If they occasionally surf the internet, they'll be more than qualified to help you in this matter. They'll have a feel for what works for them, and what they find incredibly frustrating.

26

WORKING WITH IMAGES

WHEN WORKING WITH IMAGES on the internet, there are several things that you need to think about.

Do you have the legal right to use that image? Is the image suitable for the purpose you intend to use it? Does it fit within your branding? Are you working with an image that is of the right resolution for where it's going? Is there something hidden in the metadata of the image that could be a security risk?

Let's look at each of those questions in turn.

COPYRIGHT ON IMAGES

As much as you might want to, you can't do a random Google search for any old image on the internet and use it. Photos and images, regardless of who took them, come with intellectual property rights and are protected under copyright law. And something doesn't need to be registered with a government office to be copyrighted.

Under international copyright laws, a creative work (literary, audio, and visual arts alike) has copyright protection from the moment it is in a tangible format. This includes digital formats.

Any photos that you take yourself (using your phone or other digital camera) are yours to do with as you please. *You* own the copyright. However, your rights to use images you've obtained from the internet will depend on where you've sourced those images and under what licenses.

If you are using random stock photography on your website, it is best to use images that are either in the public domain or have a creative commons license.

There are several tiers to creative commons licenses.

The lowest tier, CC0, gives you the right to do whatever you want with the image, including use it on printed commercial material, like book covers and promo material. A CC0 license means that the image is in the public domain.

A CC1 license, also called a CC BY license, also gives you the rights to do whatever you want with the image, including use it for commercial purposes, but you also need to give credit to artist or photographer of the original image.

But some creative commons licenses will restrict images to non-commercial purposes (perfect for blogging), or specify that you share the image without modification.

Be sure that you understand what the different licenses give you the rights to do with the images. For more information on creative commons licenses, visit creativecommons.org

SOURCING IMAGES WITH A CC0 LICENSE

There are many image databases on the internet filled with CC0 images. Some require a fee to download the images, while others don't.

If you choose to join a paid service, ensure that you keep copies of your receipts for the images you use. There are some scammers out there who will try to take you through the wringer, insisting that you are infringing on another person's copyright, demanding that you pay money. Victoria Strauss reported on this type of scam on her *Writer Beware* blog, detailing how these scams work and how they can catch a writer unaware. You can read the full post at:

writerbeware.blog/2023/06/23/when-the-copyright-trolls-came-for-me

However, there are several reputable *free* services that you can use too. My go-to sites for CC0 images include:

- Pixabay (pixabay.com),
- Unsplash (unsplash.com), and
- Flickr (flickr.com).

Be advised that not all images on these services are CC0 images. Before you download the image, ensure that you know exactly what restrictions are imposed on the specific image.

IMAGES CHOSEN FOR BRANDING AND PURPOSE

When choosing images to use on your website (or anywhere else on the internet), you want to choose images that not only fit within your branding, but are also fit for purpose.

Look at the base color pallet on the image. Does it compliment the colors on your website?

What about the subject matter included in the image? Does that fit within your branding themes and messaging?

When we are looking for images for a specific purpose, it's not just the color or subject matter in the image, but how busy an image is. If the image is going to be used in the background, say a background image of your website or on your promotional images for launch of your new book, you want to use images that are subtle and not too distracting. However, if you are intending to use the image as a feature image on a blog post, you want to ensure that image matches the content of the post itself, adding to the post's story.

SUITABILITY OF RESOLUTION

The ideal size for most images on web pages is around 400 pixels in width, depending on the theme you use. By restricting images to this size, you ensure that the images do not dominate the page. The smaller images also help with the load time associated with your pages.

Remember that for print-ready images, you want to be using a resolution of 300 dpi. However, for web-ready images, 90 dpi is sufficient in most cases. So, if you want that image to be 3 inches wide on the screen, then you need to use 270 pixels at a minimum. A 3-inch image intended for printed materials needs to be at least 900 pixels.

IMAGES IN WORDPRESS

WordPress has a little quirk within the image loading system. The system will automatically create multiple versions of the image file at the time the image is uploaded, each truncated to a different aspect ratio. However, the system will never scale up an image, creating image files larger than the original image.

If you upload a large image, say 1200 pixels wide (not unreasonable for a website background image), WordPress could created 10+ different copies of that image in your backend system. Normally, this isn't an issue. However, if you load a lot of images into your website (like a photographer might), this could result in too many files for your web-hosting, even if you have a small site.

Because of this quirk, it is recommended that you ensure that you upload images scaled for purpose, restricting files to the maximum size needed on your site.

METADATA ON IMAGES

Metadata is the additional bits of information added to a file that normally no one sees. For ebooks, the metadata normally includes the name of the book, the author, publisher, publication date, etc. It's the stuff used in the library part of your ereaders. For a Word file, the metadata includes the name of the creator of the file and any copyright information.

For photos, the metadata includes when the photo was taken, dimensions of the image itself in terms of pixels, and what type of camera was used in its capture, including the lens configuration if your digital camera is configured that way.

Normally, the metadata found in image files is harmless. Who cares if the photo was taken using a Nokia, a Casio, or a cellphone? That sort of information might create interesting plot twists in a novel, but that's about it. It's useless information to the average person.

However, some cameras embed GPS location information in the metadata. This is handy if you want a record of where the image was taken some years down the road. But if that photo was taken in your own home . . .

When you upload a photo to Facebook, Instagram, or other common social media sites, the metadata is often stripped from the file. Some information is used to help you generate the captions on Facebook, but once the photo is saved to your social media account, the metadata in the file itself is gone. (Though you still have the metadata in your local file.)

The same can't be said about personal websites. You upload a photo and that metadata is often preserved. It's preserved on other sites too.

People frequently share their photos on Pixabay or similar sites, embedding caption information about the subject of the image. Occasionally, the user will strip the metadata before uploading, but not always.

Here's the danger: Let's say that you took that photo inside or near your home. And let's say that your camera embedded GPS location information in the metadata. The moment you upload that photo to your website will be the moment that you share with the entire world exactly where you live. Because most people are unaware of how metadata works, most people are unaware of what details they are sharing with the public through their personal websites.

Recommendation: Take the time to understand what metadata your camera is adding to your photos. If anything looks a little dodgy, remove it from the metadata.

To access the metadata on Windows, open a *Properties* dialog for the image (right-hand click on the image), then select the *Details* tab.

On an Android phone, open the image, then tap on the 3-dot menu icon and select *Details*.

On an iPhone, open the image in your Photos app and select the *information* icon.

On a Mac, open the image in your Photos app and choose *View > Metadata*.

ALTERNATE TEXT

There are a significant number of people who use screen readers for the internet—and users of such devices are not limited to just those who have a vision impairment. I use a screen reader program that strips images and post comments (and the annoying ads) from a web page as it downloads it to my tablet to read later. And I know many writers (and editors) who take advantage of the screen reader programs as part of their editing process. (The ears detect things that the eyes don't.)

As a screen reader reads through a web page, they will read whatever happens to be in the *alternate text* for the image. If no alternate text is included, the image is skipped.

If you don't want the image to be skipped over by the screen readers, it's important that you populate the alternate text field with a useful description of the image.

Think of the alternate text as the caption in printed material. However, I need to stress that the caption in the digital world is not the same as alternate text.

The alternate text could be a description of the image itself: the text that might be shown in the image; information about the subject of the image; etc. Whereas your digital caption might be your commentary about the image.

You can populate the alternate text information on social media sites too, something that you should do, but for some social media sites, this is not as critical.

On your website, however, you can use the alternate text to help boost your SEO rankings. Put useful keywords into the alternate text, and the SEO algorithms will pick it up.

27

FORMATTING FOR THE WEB

WEBSITES AND BLOGS CONSIST of more than just words on the page. They are also a function of their typesetting and general formatting. Some care should be given to the reader experience—particularly with the internet-savvy reader.

Writing web-based content is not like writing a novel. It's a different style of writing, particularly, if you are writing informational posts like I do. The paragraphing employed is different. The sentence constructions are different. And they also employ tricks like headers and standalone sentences to get important information across.

Let's break this down, bit by bit.

TITLES NEED TO ENTICE, BUT ALSO RELATE

Let's say that you have a blog. (You do not need to have a blog, but blogging examples help me explain these concepts better.)

Writing a blog post starts with crafting the perfect title. That title needs to make a reader want to click on the link and open the post. But that title better relate to what the blog post is about.

How many times have you run a Google search (or related), and clicked on a title for a page that might be of interest, only to discover that it was an ad for some diet pill? Or what about those pages that turn out to be paragraph upon paragraph about the writer's dog when it should have been a post about the way ebooks have impacted on the publishing market? (Yeah, I actually have read a blog post like this and talk about disappointment.)

Those titles that have the entice factor but have little relevance to the post's content are known as *click-bait*. It's all about getting people to the page, because then they have your attention to sell you whatever they want.

Grr!

To craft a good title, ensure that it relates to the post, but also think about keywords that people might search for when looking for the topics covered in your post. If possible, and if the title still makes sense, use some of those keywords in the title.

For example:

- 8 Common Structural Issues Within Fiction
- Building an Email List as a Pre-published Writer
- 9 Misconceptions About Traditional Publication
- Do Titles Like Mr and Ms Still Have a Place?
- Should Social Media Be an Adult-Only Zone?
- My Daughter Hates My Instagram
- The Hologram Wants Me To Park Somewhere Else

All of these are real blog posts that I wrote at some point in the past.

White Space is Important

Many readers hate it when they encounter a blog post that is nothing but a sea of text on the page. There's not enough white space to help with readability.

This doesn't mean that you should add lots of gaps between your paragraphs or turn the background of your website to white. Many blogging engines will ignore added lines between paragraphs. And I, like so many people, find reading off a *white* screen straining on the eyes. No, what I mean by adding white space to your blog posts is to use shorter paragraphs, employ headings, and throw in the odd graphic.

Break up the text.

Think about some of the blog posts that you might have read recently. Consider their formats.

Were they easy to scan for information? Or did you have to read them in detail to understand what they were going on about? And did you like reading that detail? How fast of a read was it?

Key information needs to be structured in such a way that it can be found quickly—hence the use of headers. Any vital messages are on their own, surrounded by white space, so they stand out.

HEADERS ARE A THING

To help break up the sea of text, add a little white space by making use of headers. Even throughout this book, you will see that I've made use of headers. These headers have two roles.

1) Headers make important messages stand out.

For the reader who just skims through posts, glancing over the sea of text, the headers make important messages stand out.

Play around with the settings for H1, H2, and H3 headers. These will all look different based on the theme employed on a website, but you will find that one works better for you, attracting your eyes to the details that you would like readers to take away from your content.

2) Headers play a role in SEO searches.

It's a little SEO secret that not many writers/bloggers know about. If you put your keywords into your headers and the title of your blog posts, you will increase the chances of your posts being found in a random search.

That can't be a bad thing, right? We writers want to be found. So, if something that we can control while compiling our web pages and blog posts can improve the chances of being found, why wouldn't we do it?

However, never write content for the SEO algorithm. Everything on your website needs to be for the benefit of a human reader. What good is it to build your SEO searchable stuff if a human struggles to read the content?

Graphics Can Help, But Can Also Hinder

While graphics (and videos) can be employed to help break up the text, they also add to the load time of a web page. Image-intensive pages can be slow to load. And if it takes too long for a page to load, many readers will just give up and not bother with your content.

It frustrates me to no end when someone sends me a link for an article that I might want to read and the page lags. If that page is graphics intensive, my web browser does what it can to compensate by loading the graphics in the background, but it can still take forever—and I have a top-of-the-line machine with high-speed internet.

Graphics on a website aren't limited to just those incorporated in the page content itself. They can be found in the sidebars, headers, footers, and page backgrounds too. These all add to a page's load time.

Optimize your pages and posts to load on the slowest device and the slowest network that you have ready access to.

Graphics Impact on Reading Speed Too

For the moment, I want you to think about a time when a friend or family member came back from holiday and insisted on sharing their holiday pics with you. You start all eager and more than willing to be the captive audience, but after the third packet of photos comes out, your attention span drops away completely—that's assuming you didn't find an excuse to run for the hills after getting through only half of the first packet. And for those looking at the digital library, how many times have you tried to grab the phone out of your friend's hand so you can whiz through the remainder of the reel?

Images on web pages have the same effect. If you're anything like me, after about the fourth image, you just skim through to find the text, hunting for that one bit of information that might actually be useful.

I see it all the time. Writers have heard that images help to keep the attention of the internet reader, but they go over the top. Blog posts seem to be nothing but animated GIFs and other random images with some words scattered here and there.

What I'm trying to convey here is that one should never go over the top with images in their web pages or blog posts. The odd image here and there is helpful in breaking up the sea of text, but some people don't bother looking at all the pretty pictures.

And keep in mind those alternate text descriptions too. Those image-intensive pages will send a screen reader into overload.

If you want to use a significant number of images on your website and blog posts, go back and reread the previous chapter, and get familiar with working with images.

You Still Need to Edit

Edit the content on your web pages. Edit your blog posts. Seriously, edit them!

If you notice that you're going off topic, remove those elements. If you're starting to waffle, edit it to a concise format. Ensure that you have relevant headers and titles. Deal with your punctuation and grammatical issues. Maybe even run that post through something like Grammarly or ProWritingAid.

Think about the reader experience. There is no need to irritate prospective readers unnecessarily.

Seriously, peeps, we're writers. Part of writing is editing. We know how to do this. So, bloody well do it!

Your website is a marketing tool. If your website and blog posts are filled with typos and sentences that don't make any sense, this reflects on your writing in general.

Readers will assume that the quality of writing found on your website will be similar to that found in your published works. Of course, you and I know that this is not entirely true.

For the published works, there is commonly an editor involved somewhere during the process. Web content (and this includes blog posts) tends to be written quickly with a quick pass for editing. It's the nature of the beast.

Readers are forgiving of the odd typo here and there, but not a sea of them. So bloody well deal with them!

POPULATE THE SEO DETAILS

Most blogging and website engines give you the ability to add SEO titles and SEO description fields, even if it is only via the title of the page and the page extract. However you have access to these fields, use them.

The SEO title and description fields are what will show up in a random internet search. Make them enticing and relevant to the human at the other end of that internet search. Add keywords to your title and description fields too. But remember, they still need to make sense to a human.

If you are given a separate keywords field, populate this too. Try to be as specific as possible while not being overly specific and over-bloating the keywords.

You want those search engines to find your pages, right? Make it easy for them.

28
LEGAL OBLIGATIONS

IT DOESN'T MATTER WHERE you live. Unless you restrict your audience to just your local country and region, you are subject to international privacy laws. And these laws specify what you need to include on your websites and your newsletters.

They dictate the verbiage on our signup forms. They require that we actually have a privacy policy. And they specify where we put our contact details.

QUICK DISCLAIMER (and I now feel like a parrot): I'm not a lawyer, so you can't call this legal advice. I'm just sharing the information that I've amassed along the way.

The following discussion is pulled for the details listed in the following acts.

- The Unsolicited Electronic Messages Act 2007, New Zealand
- General Data Protection Regulation (GDPR), European Union (May 2018)
- Controlling the Assault of Non-Solicited Pornography And Marketing (CAN-SPAM), United States (December 2003)
- Canadian Anti-Spam Legislation (CASL), Canada (July 2014)
- The Spam Act 2003, Australia
- Privacy and Electronic Communications Regulations 2003, United Kingdom

I can guarantee that there will be someone out there looking at that list thinking, "I don't live there. Why does that law apply to me?"

Well . . . The GDPR protects the rights of EU citizens. If anyone who just happens to be an EU citizen visits your website, signs up your newsletters, or sends you an email, you are subject to the GDPR. It doesn't matter where in the world they live.

How can you be 100% certain that you don't have an EU citizen on your list? Are you collecting citizenship information? (My own husband is an EU citizen, so any shot I had of not having an EU citizen on my list went out the window by way of marriage.)

The CASL protects the rights of Canadian residents. Can you guarantee that you don't have a Canadian resident on your list? (Considering I have site traffic statistics that originate from Canada, I know Canadians are on my list somewhere. And one of my favorite clients is Canadian, so . . .)

I get it. It's frustrating to know that just because we live in one country we're subject to the laws of another country. This is the way of our internet world.

But it's not as complicated as I made it out to be in the beginning. Let's break this down, focusing on the key things that you need to know right away.

CONTACT INFORMATION LISTED ON YOUR WEBSITE

To be compliant with the GDPR, you must include valid contact information on your website, not just links to your social media.

If you have been paying attention to anything that I've said so far, you should already have a contact page. If not, why not? If you don't have a contact page, how can your fans send you fan mail? (You can't honestly be trying to avoid the hate mail.)

On your *Contact* page, include an email address. Yes, use a contact form, but put a valid email address that people can use to contact you too.

Just remember that any email address listed on your website might be subject to the spam bots. Accept it and move on.

(This is why I recommend using a *public-facing communications email*. Revisit chapter 4.)

PHYSICAL ADDRESSES ARE NOT CLEAR UNDER THE LAW

There are so many laws involved with postal or physical addresses. And it's not exactly clear if it is required to include a physical address on your websites or under what circumstances.

Suzanne Dibble, a data protection law expert in the UK, posted a video on this, breaking down what the law says, and how ambiguous it is. However, what she also said is that when it comes to this gray area of the law, we need to weigh up the risks. [1]

Suzanne Dibble went on to say, "I think it's advisable to have some address on [your website], so if you can, then have a virtual office where they will forward any mail to you."

This would be my recommendation as well. But remember that I'm not a lawyer. Thankfully, Suzanne Dibble is. I've included a link to her site where she talks about this issue specifically at the end of this chapter.

WEBSITES MUST INCLUDE A PRIVACY POLICY

Under the GDPR, you must make it clear exactly what data is collected from anyone who visits your website, contacts you via email, or contacts you via other means. You must also specify how that data is used.

This is your privacy policy.

So, get that privacy policy written and link it into your menus.

On my Black Wolf Editorial website, the privacy policy is linked into the menus at the bottom of the website. On my personal website, I have the privacy policy listed as a nested item under *About*.

We covered the privacy policy back in chapter 23.

SIGNUP FORMS MUST CLEARLY STATE WHAT SUBSCRIBERS ARE SIGNING UP FOR

No offense, but if you aren't doing this already, then you're crazy. You run the risk of being called a spammer. So many countries already have anti-spam laws in place, including the USA.

SIGNUP FORMS MUST CLEARLY STATE THAT SUBSCRIBERS CAN UNSUBSCRIBE AT ANY TIME

To comply with the CASL (the Canadian law), you need to include verbiage on your forms highlighting that people can unsubscribe from your email lists at any time.

I know with certainty that the default forms on MailerLite (the service I use) don't include this verbiage. I suspect the same is true of the other common email list service providers. To cover your ass, you will need to add this to your forms.

It doesn't need to be complicated.

"You can unsubscribe at any time."

Simple. Done.

I would also add a link to your privacy policy on your signup forms, assuming that you have that functionality on your form design system.

CLEAR RECORDS MAINTAINED

Clear records must be maintained, recording when subscribers opted in and how that opt-in was given.

If you are using a reputable email list management system, this will be built into the system. And it will be something that you don't need to worry about for those who use your signup forms.

If you are manually adding people to your list, be sure to add into the records additional notes about how and when you obtained *explicit permission* to add them to your email list. Document everything!

And if for whatever reason, that consent information is missing (which can happen when you move a list from one service to another), just send out a reconfirmation campaign.

I would run a reconfirm campaign on a regular basis, anyway. Tammi Labrecque of *Newsletter Ninja* fame calls this scrubbing your list. It's just one way to ensure that your email list contains only those who actually want to be on your list and open your emails.

THE RIGHT TO BE FORGOTTEN

If anyone contacts you requesting to be deleted or forgotten, you must comply. It might sound obvious, but don't be lazy with this one. Do it right away.

And *deleted* is not the same thing as *forgotten*—at least it's not in my email management system. *Deleted* will unsubscribe a person and remove their email from the database. However, *forgotten* will also remove any tracking information that reports opens or clicks. It also removes any additional tagging that was put into the MailerLite database that I don't see.

(I did mention that I use MailerLite, right?)

As a matter of habit, I tend to *forget* unsubscribers in my system.

POSTAL ADDRESS INCLUDED ON EVERY EMAIL

All emails must include an address where you can receive physical post, as in snail mail.

For security reasons, I would avoid using your home address. I use a PO Box for this purpose, but I know others who have obtained a virtual office address. To be legally compliant, all emails must have a postal address of some kind.

The nice thing here is that all reputable email list management providers have this requirement built into their systems. They collect the information needed when you set up your accounts.

Unsubscribe Method Included on Every Email

If your emails don't have this unsubscribe ability incorporated in every email, then you are sending out your emails illegally.

This is something that is built into the systems for every reputable email list management system. If you try to disable this, you can't send your emails.

Double Opt-in is Not Required, But Recommended

Under the privacy and anti-spam laws, you do not have to use *double opt-in* . . . yet. But it's a good idea to use it, anyway.

For those who don't know, a double opt-in system will send a subscriber a confirm-your-subscription email and won't add the subscriber to the email list until the confirmation has been given. By using the double opt-in, you ensure that all email addresses given are valid.

For those thinking about those free giveaways that come with newsletter subscriptions, just add your links to the first email in your onboarding automation sequence. If your email management system plan doesn't include automations, put the link on your confirmation message. Trust me, when there is a will, there is always a way.

JUST USE A REPUTABLE SERVICE . . . OKAY?

If you are using reputable service providers, they will help you to protect yourself. Their systems shouldn't let you do anything illegal, because their ass is on the line too.

As for your website, if you have forgotten to include the privacy policy or your contact details on your contacts page, it's fixable. Just go and do it now, while it's still on your mind. You can make it look pretty later. Let's just get you legally compliant first.

REFERENCES FOR THIS CHAPTER

[1] Suzanne Dibble (accessed: November, 2023) *Do you have to Disclose Your Home Address on Your Website?* https://suzannedibble.com/do-you-have-to-disclose-your-home-address-on-your-website

PART FOUR
MOUNTAIN OF BLOG

29
TO BLOG OR NOT TO BLOG

FOR YEARS, CONTENT MARKETERS have been telling writers that they should be blogging. Regular new content on your website can improve your SEO ranking.

Every time you make a change to your website (i.e., adding a page/post, deleting a page/post, changing where the links on pages/posts go to), your sitemap will change. This causes the SEO algorithms to re-index your site. The more frequently they have to re-index your site, the higher your SEO ranking. And each new blog post triggers the re-indexing of your site.

However, blogging can suck away the precious time that a writer has to write their stories.

Whether a person should blog or not really comes down to a single question: Why are you thinking about blogging?

It's time to dispel some of the myths surrounding blogging and make people face the realities before they fall into one of the many hidden traps associated with online platforms.

MISCONCEPTION #1: ALL WRITERS SHOULD HAVE A BLOG.

Why?

I can name many writers, both established and emerging, who don't blog. And there are plenty of nameless writers who have been blogging for years and still haven't gotten anywhere.

Yes, a blog with regular new content can improve SEO rankings, but for a writer who doesn't want to blog, blogging can do more harm than good.

As a writer, you need to focus your energies on the things that will help you achieve your goals, whatever those goals happen to be. For most of us, the biggest component of our goals will be directly connected to our stories and our books. This means that our stories need to come first. Activities such as social media, marketing, and blogging need to take a backseat.

But I have heard the argument that "agents and publishers want to see us blogging."

Actually, many agents and publishers don't care either way. Blogging, when used correctly, can be a powerful marketing tool. However, that's not all that agents and acquisition editors are looking at. They are more interested in the writer, their writing, and their overall marketability.

No agent worth their salt will turn you down because you don't blog. However, agents might turn you down if they see something on your blog you halfheartedly put together that they object to.

You should *never* blog just because others told you that you should. The only thing that will achieve is a sense of resentment and failure when you don't meet your blogging objective.

If you don't want to blog, then DON'T DO IT!

MISCONCEPTION #2: BLOGGING IS A QUICK WAY TO BUILD A FOLLOWING.

Now that I've fallen out of my chair laughing so hard . . .

Perhaps when the internet was still in its early days, this was the case, but in today's internet world, the number of blogs out there is insane. Everyone is competing to be heard.

I have been blogging since 2014. It took me nearly five years to reach triple digits with my subscriber numbers. A decade after I first started blogging, and I'm still nowhere near to breaking the four-digit barrier.

Whoever decided that blogging was the quickest way to build a following was on the coo-coo bus.

I don't tell you this because I don't want you to blog. If you want to blog, then do it. However, accept the fact that in the beginning, you will be blogging for yourself. Eventually, you'll build an audience who gets you, with readers flocking to anything that you write, but blogging is part of the long-term game.

In the beginning, post it, and listen to the crickets make music.

MISCONCEPTION #3: POST IT AND THEY WILL COME.

This is just another way of phrasing Misconception #2.

Maybe the idea of "build it and they will come" works for baseball, but it certainly doesn't work for blogging.

To truly build a following, you need to spread the word about your blog's existence. You need to market it, shouting it out on various social media channels. But just like those book ads, you can't be 100% on the "read my blog" train. You need to mix up the messages.

Even then, it can still feel like you're shouting into the void.

MISCONCEPTION #4: BLOG ABOUT WHAT YOU KNOW . . . AND WRITERS KNOW ABOUT WRITING.

There are two different aspects to this one. Let's start with how writers should write about what they know.

The assumption here is that writers should write about writing because it's what we know. However, writers know about a lot of things, and we learn more every day. Writers are skilled researchers!

But there are some who still hold fast to the idea that writers should blog about writing.

Why? What is the purpose? There are a lot of blogs out there about writing.

Writers who blog should produce content targeting the type of reader that they're trying to attract. Unless you have a strategic business reason to be blogging about writing, then don't waste your time.

Yes, I blog about writing, but there is a business reason for it. The site blackwolfeditorial.com is for my editorial business—that's its primary function—providing a portal for writers to contact me about editorial and writing coaching services. The blog is there to service that business, providing useful information about editing and publishing. Everything about that blog is targeted at writers, attempting to drum up business.

At every step of the way, including in those beginning stages and through your social media interactions, think about who your ideal reader is. Share the content that they would like.

I'm guessing that your ideal readership consists of more than just writers. So, you need to write about the topics that will connect with your readers.

I once chatted with someone via social media about this topic. When I asked what they're an expert at, they answered, "I'm an expert on dreaming and that's about it." I wanted to reach my hands through my monitor to hug her—and slap her silly.

She was an expert on dreaming. Perfect! There is no better way to connect with others than to write about hopes and dreams and the steps taken to achieve those goals. But to say that's all she knew? Really?

So, she knows nothing about what it's like to juggle the life of being a mother, and stealing those precious moments needed to write or edit? So, she knows nothing about what it's like to be a wife of a husband who is never home? She never feels self-doubt or insecurity?

"But people don't want to read about that."

If that was the case, then why are there so many mommy blogs out there, many of them with large followings? People want to know that they're not alone in their struggles. It's always reassuring to see how others deal with the daily chaos of life.

For my personal blog (found at judylmohr.com), the target audience is anyone willing to listen. That may sound incredibly broad, but the posts are a mishmash of thoughts and topics. I write about the emotional roller coaster that writing is. I occasionally throw in my thoughts about raising two young adults (who are now legal adults, but I certainly wouldn't call them self-sufficient). I have posts about science, technology, and where things can go horribly wrong. And there are random thoughts that seem to have no connection to anything else, like why I hate the term *aspiring writer*.

My personal blog is a diary about my personal journey. If others get something out of it, great. If they don't, who cares? I write those posts for my benefit, because if I don't get them out, my mind continues to harp on them until I do.

Misconception #5: Blogs should be about a single topic.

Bwahahaha . . . Seriously, peeps, if you believe this one, then you really need to go look at the archives on both of my blogs.

Yes, a blog needs to have a theme, but guess what? *You* are your blog's theme. If you honestly feel that you are an expert at nothing, then make your blog all about *you* and *your writing*.

Include information about your journey into this publishing world. Possibly include interesting facts that you've discovered during your research.

Someone who writes for the millennial generation might have pieces that are more heavily slanted to social topics, with strong opinions on those topics. The nonfiction writer who writes about medieval cultures might write posts about historical research, including photos of ancient relics. And the children's writer might be whimsical with what they post, keeping it age appropriate to their readers.

Write about what you want to write about—and the naysayers can just suck it up and deal with it.

MISCONCEPTION #6: FOR A BLOG TO BE SUCCESSFUL, YOU NEED TO BLOG DAILY.

Where does one even begin with this one?

Some content marketers have been pushing this idea for a long time, rightly pointing out that it helps to boost SEO rankings. To make it easier for people, some so-called experts advocate that you post "cat pictures" and other random things that add zero value, just so you can have new content.

No matter how you look at it, this comes down to the quality-vs-quantity argument. Lots of new content will increase visibility of a website, but only for a while. Eventually, readers will seek quality content. Those random cat memes might be good for social media feeds, but on a blog, where you have more space to properly formulate your thoughts and where archives stick around much longer, it might not be enough.

Bloggers, particularly bloggers who are writers of longer works, should produce longer blog posts—within reason. However, the longer something is, the longer it takes to craft and edit.

Blogging every day is a huge ask and a massive time sink. I speak from experience. I've tried it—and I burnt out!

Focus your energies on the works that you want to share with the world. If you want to be a novelist, focus on writing novels. If you want to be a blogger, then go ahead and write that daily blog post.

And I'll be sitting in the corner with the wine, waiting for you to come to your senses.

MISCONCEPTION #7: BLOGS NEED TO BE SHORT.

The length of a blog post depends on the nature of the post itself. I have seen some posts that are 500 words or less. Others easily clock in at 3000 words. The bulk of my blog posts come in somewhere between 1000 to 2000 words, sometimes longer.

Confused yet?

Just like everything else we write, there is no right or wrong when it comes to length. However, there will be a point where a post is too short or too long. It feels incomplete or like it's dragging.

The average internet-based reader has a short attention span. Don't waffle on about the one topic for page after page. Edit your blog posts with the same care that you would edit your other writing.

Misconception #8: You shouldn't spend more than an hour writing your blogs.

Actually, this one isn't a misconception. This one is practical, sound advice.

I said it when responding to the first misconception listed in this chapter. As a writer, you need to focus your energies on the things that will help you achieve your goals, whatever those goals happen to be. Activities such as social media, marketing, and blogging need to take a backseat.

So, limiting the time you spend writing and editing your blog posts gives you more time to work on your other writing.

For my own blog post, I often do my initial writing and editing within an hour (or two), then leave it for a day. When I come back to the post, I often find copyediting errors and clunky sentences that I missed in my rush the day before. And I inevitably find a typo after the post has gone live too. It's the nature of the beast. The nice thing about blogging is that you can easily go in after the post is live and edit that typo.

CONSISTENCY IS THE KEY

The real trick to blogging, in a sane manner that can be managed, is to blog about topics that interest you, and to be consistent about when you release new material. If that means releasing a new blog post once a month, so be it.

Take advantage of scheduling tools. I often go on a blog-writing binge once every few months, and stack those blog posts up for three to four months, then forget about my blogs for a while. Then I can focus on my other projects until I need to have another blog-writing binge.

When all is said and done, you shouldn't listen to the content marketers when it comes to blogging.

Blog only if you want to.

Blog about topics that interest you, attracting your ideal reader—who is probably similar to you, so they'll be interested in what you are interested in.

And if you do decide to blog, be consistent about it, but be sensible about it too.

Don't try to be a machine.

30
GUEST BLOGGING

BLOGGING ON A REGULAR basis is not for everyone. But blogging is a powerful marketing tool when used in the right way. Regardless if you have a blog where you post regularly or whether you elect to avoid blogging on your own accounts, I would recommend that you consider guest blogging occasionally.

Guest blogs can be a great way to get your name out there as a writer. Most blog hosts will allow you to have links to your various online accounts, and are happy to include a brief bio and profile picture. And many guest blogging opportunities will also come with the ability to include something about your latest book. For the time and effort it takes to write that blog post, you get free advertising.

However, there are some rules you should follow when it comes to pitching guest blog posts.

DO YOUR RESEARCH

Just like pitching a manuscript to an agent or publisher, you need to do your research. You have one question that you're seeking answers to: Is the blog in question somewhere you would be happy to have your work posted?

Your name is going to be attached to an article on that blog, possibly for all time—at least until the blog host either takes your page down or the entire site down. As such, you need to ensure that you would be happy to have your name associated with that site. You might have other questions, such as site traffic, marketing, etc. It really comes down to the site and the blog itself.

1) Look at the site layout. Is it easy to find things?
2) If your article was listed there, would readers be able to easily find it, or would it become quickly buried, never to see the light of day?
3) Can *you* navigate the site?
4) Is the site riddled with broken links?
5) When was the last time any of the pages were actually updated? (Yes, you can get that information just from looking at a site.)

What about the site theme? Is it something that someone just slapped together with no thought about the reader experience, or has some time and effort been put into the site pages?

I've turned down a guest blog opportunity because the site used such a hideous theme and was poorly laid out.

With sites such as WordPress.com and Weebly.com, there really isn't any excuse for a website to have a horrid theme. Yet, I still encounter sites where the chosen theme is inappropriate or not customized to suit the blogger. This results in posts that are never seen and links to other online platforms that disappear. A little time and effort is all it takes, and it shows within the final result.

READ THE BLOG FIRST

Say that you're happy with the site itself, but what about the blog? Read through a few of the entries. You don't need to read through the entire archive, but after reading a few posts, you should be able to determine the underlying theme. You'll want to do this for multiple reasons.

1) Is the content of the blog something that you would be happy to be associated with?
2) Do you have something of value to contribute to the blog?
3) Does the tone of the blog posts suit your writing style?
4) Would readers of the blog be interested in your other work?

Look at it critically. Guest blogging is a marketing tool for your other writing. You need to ensure that every post you have out there will eventually drive the right type of reader to your other stuff.

FOLLOW SUBMISSION GUIDELINES

Let's say that you've found the perfect blog and you know exactly what you could contribute. Now what?

Some sites openly advertise for submissions for guest blog posts. Pay attention to the submission guidelines, just like you would for submission to an agent or publisher. However, submissions to blogs aren't as tightly regulated, and the process is much faster and often more laid-back. Some sites will offer money for guest posts, but, if they do, they will specify this on the site along with the submission guidelines. If no mention is made of financial remuneration, then it's safe to assume that there isn't any.

If the site you're interested in doesn't have submission guidelines listed, then you will need to contact the web administrator directly. Keep the initial contact professional. Give them a brief (one or two sentence) description of the proposed post. DO NOT send a copy of the post until invited to do so.

Ensure What You Pitch is What You Send

You've done your research. You've found the perfect blog. You've pitched a blog idea to them, and they've invited you to send them the full post for review. What you send them better be what you pitched.

It looks bad on you, and can be damaging to your reputation, if you had pitched a post about how to deal with rejection but sent a recipe for a chocolate cake instead—unless you're making an analogy between that chocolate cake recipe and rejection. It doesn't matter how well written that chocolate cake recipe is; they were expecting insights on how to deal with rejections. And guess what? You are now dealing with rejection yourself.

The Opportunities are Endless

I have written a few guest blog post myself for various websites. In some cases, I was approached by the blog host for the article, and I happily wrote one for them. (My post about holograms on Dan Koboldt's site (found at dankoboldt.com/holograms-science-fiction-writing) was one of these, and it was an article that I loved writing.) My interactions on social media have led to invitations from various directions. I have been asked to write about science, writing, and editing. The opportunities are endless.

Guest blogging is not something to be afraid of. You never know where it could lead.

PART FIVE
NEWSLETTERS AND EMAIL LISTS

31
THE NEEDED EMAIL LIST

ALL OF FIVE YEARS ago, I would have said that it didn't really matter if you had an email list or not. In recent times, I have been shown the light.

It doesn't take much for social media to implode and the landscape to suddenly change. Just think about the mass exodus from Twitter (sorry, I mean X) since Elon Musk took over.

And I've lost count of the number of times Facebook has changed their algorithms. I swear my posts get lost in the void, never to be seen by the masses.

There was a time when I couldn't share links to my blog posts on Facebook. It wasn't anything that I did—I wasn't in Facebook jail—but it had to do with policies regarding Australian news sites. Somewhere in the confusion, no one was able to link to anything on an Australian news site on the platform. And somehow, my website got caught up in the mess. I don't totally understand what happened, because I don't write news, and I'm not in Australia, but Facebook had tagged my domain as Australian news. Hence, no links to the site could be shared. It was frustrating, but it also hammered home the point that social media could disappear within the blink of an eye.

Relying on social media to market your books, to reach your audience, is a disaster waiting to happen.

The one form of internet-based marketing that has stood the test of time, surviving all of the social media nightmares, is email marketing. This means that your best avenue of marketing your books (and your services if you are a service provider) is to maintain an email list. That email list gives you a direct line of communication with your readers, without the algorithms getting in the way.

Think about your own activities and the way you react to things.

If you're on X, do you take the time to read through every single tweet sent out by everyone that you follow? Of course not. If you did, you wouldn't have time for anything else. Instead, you apply a level of self-filtering, either by way of lists or hashtag searches. There might be a handful of people whose profile you actively visit, but that's about it.

Those on Facebook frequently complain about the changes made to the algorithm for the main feed. You might have enjoyed reading the comments from one of your *friends*, but they suddenly go silent and you don't know why. You go and look at their feed, and they've actually been active, but you haven't seen any of their updates. Facebook has taken it upon themselves to decide what you want to see—never mind that they might get it wrong.

Think about all the blogs that you might follow. Have you got every single one bookmarked? How long is the bookmark list? How many of those blogs do you actually read? Be honest with yourself.

Now think about your email. How often do you check your email? Do you read all your emails? Do you scan through the subjects and the senders at least? How many times has something in those subject lines or sender IDs caught your eye? Have you clicked on links in the email and kept reading on a website to find out more?

Those in marketing have learned that if you want to get the attention of your readers, you need to get into their email inboxes. Email lists is it, baby.

Now, here is the downside. Maintaining an email list also means sending out emails on a regular basis.

Use a Third-Party Email List Management Service

Yes, if you are really lazy, you could have your blogging engine maintain your email list for you. Those using WordPress could have people subscribe to their blogs that way, with the subscribers list maintained by the WordPress engine. However, this is a dangerous idea.

What if something happens to your website and you lose access to it (worst-case scenario)? You then lose access to your subscribers, and you have to start over again.

It's safer to maintain an email list that is separate from your web-hosting provider. Use a reputable email list service.

At the time of writing this book, MailerLite was the best option out there that provided a *free* account to writers, giving you the ability to send automations and fully customize the look and feel of your emails and forms.

I'm not going to go into the nitty-gritty of creating email lists, building your following through email lists, or how to generate the perfect freebie giveaway. Instead, I'm going to point you in the direction of Tammi Labrecque, also known as the *Newsletter Ninja* (newsletterninja.net).

Tammi is an expert in email marketing for writers. I employ many of her ideas and philosophies myself within my own email lists. Trust me, when it comes to email lists for writers, Tammi is the one you want to follow.

But I do want to take some time to point out some of the security issues, legalities, and system quirks associate with email lists in general.

32

ADMINISTRATION AND LEGALITIES

WE COVERED SOME OF the legal stuff when we spoke about the privacy policy and other things legally required to be present on your website (in chapters 23 and 28). As a reminder:

1) Contact information must be listed on your website, not just social media links.
2) Postal addresses on your website are recommended (their legal requirement is ambiguous).
3) Your website must include a privacy policy.
4) Your signup forms must clearly state what subscribers are signing up for.
5) Your signup forms must clearly state that subscribers can unsubscribe at any time.
6) Clear records must be maintained, recording when subscribers opted in and how that opt-in was given.
7) You must comply with the removal of subscribers.
8) Every email sent to your list must include a physical postal address.
9) An unsubscribe method must be included in every email.
10) Double opt-in is not required, but is recommended.
11) Use the appropriate SSL certificate for your website.

Yeah, it's a lot to remember. Well, here are some more things to remember.

Emails Associated with List Administration

Back in chapter 4, we discussed the emails that writers will want to have to protect their systems. If you decided to skim over that chapter, I highly recommend that you go back and read it. But for those of you who can't be bothered . . .

For security purposes, you will want to *log in* to your email list management system using one of your secret-squirrel *administration emails*. However, you will want to send out emails using a *public-facing communications email*.

That's two (2) email addresses that are going to be associated with your email list administration.

Unsubscribe Doesn't Mean Forgotten

Just because a person unsubscribes from one list doesn't necessarily mean that they have been removed from your lists. And when you are paying per subscriber, it's important to know exactly who is subscribed and who isn't.

As a matter of habit, when I check my subscribers list (downloading a copy of the latest list), anyone listed as *unsubscribed* gets deleted (or forgotten) from the system. However, deleted is not necessarily the same as forgotten.

On MailerLite, forgotten means that the stats associated with a particular email are also removed from the system. Deleted will remove a person's email, but the open statistics are preserved.

Side Note about Mailchimp

For a long time, Mailchimp was the email list provider of choice for many writers, but that changed years ago when Mailchimp changed their policies around who was included in the subscriber totals and who wasn't.

At some point, Mailchimp got the bright idea to change their charges based on the number of *contacts* you had listed on each sublist. If a subscriber was listed in multiple groups (or sublists), then they counted multiple times to your *contacts* total. And those who were no longer subscribed but were still listed in your system also counted. So, you could easily be paying for those who you legally couldn't send an email to just because they were still in your database. (Hence why I delete those who unsubscribe.)

There were other things that went wrong with Mailchimp too. Let's just say that if you ask who writers prefer to use for their mailing list, you would be hard pressed to find anyone who recommends Mailchimp.

NOT ALL SUBSCRIPTIONS NEED BE VIA ONLINE FORM

It is easiest from a mailing list management perspective if your subscribers use one of your funky online forms that you've spent hours designing. Not only do they get to see the pretty choices that you've made for your branding, but the systems will record the opt-in information (a legal requirement).

However, there might be times when someone sends you an email asking to be added to your list. Or maybe you've presented at an in-person workshop and got people to sign up by way of pen and paper.

All reputable systems will allow you to manually add a person to your list. Just make a note in the records for that subscriber exactly when and how the consent was given. Keep records of everything!

KEEP BACKUPS BY DOWNLOADING CSV FILES

There is always the risk that you could lose access to one or more of your systems. Something could happen to your email. Or maybe your email management provider changes things, limiting your access. Or maybe you're in the middle of restructuring and decide to move from one provider to another.

On a regular basis, download a copy of your subscriber list by downloading a CSV file. This file can be opened in any spreadsheet program, but more importantly, you have your full list of subscribers if something happens and you need to start again. With that CSV in hand, you won't be starting from scratch.

I set a task reminder to download the latest subscriber list once a month. And I tuck the file away in my monthly backups for my computer.

List Health

To help maintain your list's health, you will want to run re-engagement campaigns and occasionally scrub your lists.

Re-engagement campaigns are those automated sequences that pick up when a subscriber is no longer engaging with your emails (opening them and clicking things). The idea is that by using a targeted campaign, you will hopefully encourage them to re-engage with your content.

However, sometimes you need to scrub your list. If you have too many people on your list who aren't opening emails or engaging with your content in some fashion, this can have a negative impact on the way Google and other email providers treat your emails. You could suddenly find yourself being tagged as promotions, or worse, flagged as spam.

It is much better to have a small list that is engaged with your emails than to have a large list with low open rates.

Leader Magnets and Onboarding Sequences

Leader magnets are those little freebies that you give away when people sign up for your email list. Among writers, it is common to give away a short story or novella, but that isn't necessary.

Karen Slaughter (a successful thriller writer) gives away case file notes (fancy documents created from her writing notes) to accompany her books. Alex Scarrow (author of the *Time Riders* series) used to use character interviews for his leader magnets. And some fantasy writers use maps of their worlds.

The ideas are only limited by your imagination. Feel free to multi-purpose something that you needed to create for yourself.

Once you have decided on the perfect leader magnet, you'll need to think about your onboarding sequence (i.e., the automated emails used to welcome new subscribers to your list).

If you want to dive into the nitty-gritty of onboarding sequences and email automations, you should follow Tammi Labrecque (author of *Newsletter Ninja*). She has classes and workshops on building those automations. She's the queen of email marketing for writers.

One of the things that Tammi recommends (and I agree) is to use tags and groups to keep track of which pathway a subscriber came through to be on your list. Not only will this help you identify which leader magnets are working, but it also gives you the ability to easily segment your list and send targeted emails.

I'm going to say it again, because I can't recommend her enough. Follow Tammi Labrecque (*Newsletter Ninja*). Get her books. Join her Facebook group. Trust me on this one. She's the one who is in the know on this stuff!

POSTING FREQUENCY

There are multiple schools of thought on this one. I know of some authors who like to send daily emails (why, I'll never fully understand, because it seems like so much hard work for very little gain). There are others who send out emails weekly. Some send out bi-weekly. I send out monthly newsletters to my lists. And I subscribe to a few lists who send out things only when they have something to say.

What it comes down to is brand recognition and how much mental bandwidth you have to dedicate to email marketing.

If you are one of those who wants to send out something only when you have something to say, ensure that you have the name to back it up. If a person gets a random email from a name they don't recognize, your email will be instantly flagged as spam, and you will likely have a large number of *unsubscribes* or *never reads*. That name recognition is the only thing that will save you at that point.

For the bulk of us who are just trying to build the lists and get noticed, the key is consistency at a frequency that we can safely manage and not too long between emails that our subscribers forget who we are. Give yourself room for life to get in the way (because life is always getting in the way). Don't pick such a rigid schedule that you are going to stress yourself out.

For the sake of sanity (for both yourself and your readers), I wouldn't send out daily emails. For the daily stuff, take it to social media. This is because most people don't bother reading daily emails—they have other, more important things to do. So, when you send out the one email filled with the important stuff, people will likely miss it, because they're used to ignoring your emails.

Once a week is the maximum frequency that I would send emails out. Pick a day of the week and stick with it. But weekly emails can be a big commitment.

If you think you can safely send out weekly emails, then possibly send them out bi-weekly. If you think you can safely do bi-weekly, then send them out monthly.

Bi-monthly or quarterly is probably the minimum frequency I would pick. A lot can change in a two-month or three-month period. Those emails would likely get long. And readers will likely put the email into another folder to read later . . . and later never comes.

I think the bi-weekly or monthly frequency works best. It's long enough between emails that things can change, giving you something to actually include, but it's not too long that you run the risk of people forgetting who you are. But when it comes to deciding which one to go with, look at your schedule and be honest with yourself about how much time you need to craft those newsletters.

I maintain two newsletter email lists for the same reason that I maintain two blogs. Audiences are different. But for the sake of my mental sanity, I only send out monthly newsletters for each list. I don't have the mental bandwidth to do anything more frequent.

IMAGES AND HEADERS IN EMAILS

Again, there are many schools of thought on this one. At one point, headers and images were all the rage. Now email marketers are suggesting that you use plain-text emails only.

My suggestion: You do you!

Look at the newsletters of those you follow. Make a list of what you like about them and what you don't like. Use that as your starting point for your own email design. If you set up the expectation of your readers for one format, they'll get used to it and will happily go with what you want to do.

Remember that images affect the time it takes to load an email into an email reader. Keep any images small within email if you use them. (Thankfully, most of the email management providers have this particular aspect built into their systems.)

BE KIND TO YOURSELF AND YOUR READERS

If you are struggling to get newsletters out, be open and honest and tell your readers this. You don't need to go into the details of your busy life, but by keeping the lines of communications open, you remind your readers that you're human and not some artificial intelligence. (Given today's environment, that's got to be a good thing, right?)

I know it's a lot to remember. But the first step in any process is to breathe. If you don't breathe, you'll go blue in the face, and not a nice bright blue either—it'll be that icky gray-blue.

33

AVOIDING THE SPAM FILTER

IN RECENT TIMES, GOOGLE and Yahoo, the biggest two providers of free emails, made announcements that will impact on the deliverability of emails from email lists. If you are using a reputable email management system (which you should be), then you will already be in the know regarding this. Providers like MailerLite, Active Campaign, Mailchimp, etc. all need to ensure that their clients are still able to do email marketing. However, just in case you decided to ignore those emails from your email list management system, we better go through these changes. Some of them will have a significant impact on the budgets for many writers.

I apologize in advance for the technical nature of this chapter, but there is no way of avoiding it. Setting up emails to avoid the spam filters requires some funky computer magic in the backend of systems. Even then, you can still get it wrong. Yeah, this is something else I speak about from experience, and I'm still suffering the consequences of the stupid things I did.

REQUEST SUBSCRIBERS "WHITE LIST" YOUR EMAIL

As part of your welcome email, possibly even as part of your signup *thank you*, ask your subscribers to "white list" your email. This will be something within their email hosting system (and yes, Gmail has white listing too). Within their system, an email user can specify which emails are lovingly deposited into the inbox regardless of what the spam filter says.

The white list is a spam filter bypass that is controlled by the receiving email. However, how a user adds an email address to the white list is different for every email editor program.

Hubspot has a useful blog post that contains pictorial instructions on how to white list an email in the commonly used email systems. Be advised that the instructions might be out of date due to interface updates. The blog post in question can be found at:

blog.hubspot.com/marketing/email-whitelist

ADD A SIGNATURE TO EMAILS

All emails you send out should include some sort of signature at the bottom, even your general communications emails.

Most of us do this instinctively, even if it's just our names. However, I would recommend that you add a bit more. It doesn't need to be much more, just something to add your contact details . . . which, if you remember, is a legal requirement for your newsletters, anyway. Why not add it to your general emails too?

POPULATE THE REPLY-TO FIELD

If you are using a reputable email management system, this won't be an issue for your newsletter emails. This is done automatically. However, the deliverability of your general communications emails could be negatively impacted if you leave this field empty.

Take a look at your account settings in your favored email editor program (i.e., Outlook, Thunderbird, Apple Mail, Gmail). All email editor programs give you the ability to add something to the *reply-to* field. And it's something that you can change at the time you send individual emails.

Normally, the reply-to field is something that is used when you want replies to go to an email address that differs from the email you're sending things from. If this field is empty, email programs assume that all replies are to go to the sending email.

Spam filters are now looking at this field. If it's empty, it's one negative point against the email and a slightly higher chance that it could be flagged as spam.

So, even if you are copying your sending address into the field, populate that reply-to field in your email editor. If you populate it in your account settings, then *all* emails you send out will have that field populated by default.

One-click Unsubscribes are Required

This one is easy to manage, because if you are using a reputable email list management system, this will be handled for you.

However, for those who might be running different newsletters to different email lists from the same system, you might have an issue. You may need to separate out your accounts.

For most of us, this won't be an issue, because for most writers, managing one newsletter is more than enough to send us to the brink of insanity.

Emails Must Come From Authenticated Domains

Gone are the days of being able to send your emails (if you are just starting out) from a free email like Gmail.

While it has been recommended that your sending domains be authenticated for some time, from February 2024, Google and Yahoo made it a requirement.

But what does this mean?

Well, writers with an email list must now have their own custom domain. *And* you must have an email address attached to that custom domain (e.g., sally@sallywrites.com).

But to have your domain *authenticated*, you need to be able to access the DNS record to make changes. And to have access to the DNS records, you need to be self-hosted.

And the budgets for many writers just went through the roof.

(By the way, DNS stands for Domain Name System. Not an imaginative name, if you ask me. No wonder everyone just calls it DNS. It sounds so much *smarter* and *mysterious*.)

But let's say that you're already self-hosted with a custom domain email. Your third-party email management system will provide you with the information that you need to add to your DNS records for your domain to become authenticated. Just contact your hosting provider to get technical support on adding information to your DNS records.

There will be a few strings that you'll need to add to the DNS records to avoid the spam filters. And unfortunately, you won't get all of the strings at the same time . . . So, this whole process may take multiple calls to technical support.

DOMAIN ALIGNMENT WILL BE REQUIRED

Once your domain is *authenticated*, you can set up domain alignment. This will require a few more records to be added to your DNS records. Again, your email management system will provide you with the strings needed, so technical support for your hosting provider should be able to help you with this.

Just so you know, domain alignment also makes the links embedded in your emails look like they are directly attached to your domain. It's kind-of neat how that happens.

DMARC Records Will Be Required

For those with large email lists, you will also need to set up what is known as a DMARC or Domain-based Message Authentication, Reporting and Conformance.

(Seriously, where is the imagination in naming these things? Clearly, they weren't writers.)

The DMARC record in your DNS tells any external system that you're not a bot, but are a legit business using legitimate emails. It's just one of many things that you can do to ensure that you are not seen as a phishing scam or pretending to be someone else. (Well, you can still be pretending to be someone else, but the email systems don't know that.)

The information needed for this does not come from your email management system. This one is specific to your hosting provider. It is best that you get technical support on this one.

Don't go poking around in systems that you don't fully understand. (Yeah, been there and done that too. Oopsie! At least I can laugh about it, and thank goodness that technical support was able to do something about the mess I had made. I know I've already said this, but oopsie!)

Workaround For Those Who Can't Afford Self-hosting

I'm not normally one to recommend services without knowing the ins and outs of how that service works, especially if I've never used the system myself. But I can't just leave those unable to afford self-hosted websites without a way to having an email list.

If you fall into this category, unable to afford your own domain, look into Substack.

Substack is more of a blogging system, but many writers (and other creatives) have taken to using the system to generate their newsletters. For one, you can monetize your newsletters, but more importantly for this argument, Substack uses its own authenticated domain for sending out notifications and newsletters to your subscribers. While you can add a custom domain to your "blog" for lack of a better term, the emails don't come from your domain.

I'm not a hundred percent certain how one might manage list health on Substack, ensuring that your list contains the email addresses of only those who *want* to receive your emails. And I'm not sure how you might manage the freebie giveaways either. I don't use Substack myself. But it is a workaround to this custom domain issue.

TEST EMAILS FOR "SPAMMYNESS"

Mail-tester is a free online service that you can use to test the *spammyness* of your emails (their term, not mine). When you first load the site (found at mail-tester.com), it gives you a randomly generated email address to send the email you want tested to. It then runs a report on your email and comes back with a list of things that you can do to help improve your *spam health*. Some fixes are super easy. Others require some technical know-how (or a phone call to technical support).

Even with everything in place, you might still find the spam folder. I know that my emails do, and it's frustrating in the extreme.

PART SIX
THE SOCIAL MEDIA BEAST

34
Navigating the Social Media Maze

There are many social media marketing experts who will spout off all the reasons why you should sign up to this network or that one, professing that if you spend the time, effort, and energy in building an active presence on a given network, you will have great returns. Some will even promise that you will see an increase in sales of X%. No offense, but X% increase in sales when you have zero sales in the first place will be a promise fulfilled. Yet, it is common to see those annoying "Buy my book" ads on the various channels.

Social media is called social media for a reason—because it's meant to be social. Social media is good for only one thing: connecting with others.

Facebook, Instagram, Mastodon, X, and every other platform out there are designed to interact with others and foster connections. They are networking tools.

If you put lots of time into social media, you'll likely see very little financial return. In fact, you might not see any gains at all.

I hear you asking—shouting really—"What's the point?"

Look back at the paragraphs above.

> Social media is about fostering connections.

Without those connections, you will struggle in a big way to get the word out there. You need help. You can't do it alone.

To be successful in your social media marketing efforts, the first thing you need to do is stop thinking of social media as marketing, because it's not. Think about it as an opportunity to meet others, making contacts that could lead to other opportunities.

The next step in building a presence on social media is to focus your efforts on the networks you enjoy.

Let's be honest here . . . If we signed up for every site in existence with the intent to actively use those accounts, we would either come across as a fully automated bot, or we would spend so much time on social media that we would never get any writing done.

There is an old saying that couldn't be truer when it comes to social media and an online presence: It's better to do one thing well than to do a half-assed job on multiple things. Don't spread yourself too thinly.

Yes, you can link social media sites together, but if you link things incorrectly, you can look like a dweeb who can't string three words together to form a sentence. Definitely not a good look for a writer. And if you use automation too heavily, you look like a bot.

Social media is meant to be social; it's intended to make those valuable connections. If you automate accounts, linking them to others, then when exactly will you interact with followers and build connections? Yes, you'll have an active online presence, but is that presence doing you more harm than good?

Instead of signing up to every social media site in existence, it is best to select one or two social media sites and focus your efforts on those, removing the automation and doing things the good old-fashioned way—manually. The manual approach means that you will be signing into a given account regularly and interacting with your followers.

Now for the do-as-I-say-not-as-I-do routine.

Personally, I'm the most active on Facebook and Discord. My other accounts have the occasional posts from me and a bit of interaction, but not often. It's when I remember to log in.

For sites like LinkedIn, I rely on automations and those emails that tell me someone has sent me a message. My X accounts used to be connected to my blogs, with tweets going out every time a new blog post went live, but somewhere along the line, X decided to break those connections with Jetpack (the WordPress plugin that provides the publicize features, among other things).

I used to share a lot of sunrise photos on Instagram, but editing those photos so they were suitable to post on the site became a chore and sucked the joy out of sunrise photography. For Threads and Mastodon . . . I'm still trying to figure out how best to utilize the sites and how they fit within my platform.

Basically, except for Facebook and Discord (both of which I'm on every day), I set weekly reminders telling me to log in to my accounts, send posts, and respond to messages. If you happen to catch me while I'm in there, I'll happily interact and chat with you. But most of the time, it's random.

The trick to sanity here is to focus only on the sites that work best for you. But how does one choose the social media sites appropriate for oneself?

To answer that question, we need to look at the different sites and determine what they are intended for.

WHAT IS GOOD FOR WHAT?

There are an insane number of social media sites out there and more keep cropping up every day. Before you embark on the journey of any social media site, there is a list of questions that you need to ask yourself.

1) Does my personality fit this social media site?
2) Will the site fill a need that my other accounts don't?
3) Do I actually have the time required to service and maintain an account for this site?
4) What is the plan for content on the account?

5) How often do I need to post to the account to build a following and gain attention?

6) Do I have the budget to build the account? (Think about both the cost in dollars and the cost in time.)

7) What is the goal of the account? How will I know if it's successful?

8) Why should I spend time on this particular account instead of other marketing activities?

Everything you do should always come back to your long-term goals. If you want to be the next Dr. Seuss, then sites like X and Threads will be a waste of time.

Let's take a brief look at the more popular options.

FACEBOOK

Facebook is designed for longer messages, using complete sentence structures. The site is the ideal network for discussion groups and connecting with other writers or those with similar interests. Because there is little restriction on the length of posts, if you are stuck on a problem, you can provide full details and get valuable feedback.

Yes, Facebook can be used as a marketing tool for new (and old) books, but before you spend the money on Facebook ads, you should be aware that Facebook has made changes to their news feed algorithms. Your posts might not find the feeds of your target audience.

Regardless of the annoying things that Facebook has done with the standard news feeds, because of the networking features alone, Facebook is a valuable social media site for networking and building writing communities.

Biggest Risk Associated with Facebook

When looking at the security associated with Facebook, you need to be aware that Facebook is notorious for changing their settings at the drop of a hat. Every time you see a change in the interface, assume that something else has changed under the hood. Dig through *all* settings to see what has changed, and verify that you are using the settings that are right for you.

X (Formerly Known as Twitter)

X's short message nature (280 characters for the accounts on the lowest tier at the time this book was written) has made this site ideal for those who don't have a lot of time to carefully construct a full post. With a quick hashtag search, you can narrow your feed to just the information you want to see, but you are not limited to just the other accounts you follow.

Conversations, for the most part, are on public display, generating more interest from those who use the site.

The writing and publishing community on X was once strong. Over recent years, the site has seen a lot of changes (and not just the name of the site). The changes have made the writing community nervous and uncertain about the future of the platform. Many writers left the platform in late 2022, and more writers left when it was suggested that the platform would become a pay-to-play site for users.

Some agents and publishers are still active on the site, posting information about their manuscript wish lists (#MSWL). You can also find other tidbits about querying, editing, and writing. However, exactly how long the writing community will remain on the site is questionable.

Biggest Risk Associated with X

X has made a significant number of changes to their system since Elon Musk took over in November 2022. If you are on the site, ensure that you know what all of those settings do, and be sure that you are making the full use of the features that you have access to. (The two-factor authentication features are restricted on the lowest-tier accounts.)

INSTAGRAM

Instagram is the perfect playground for anyone who takes lots of photos and wants to share them with the world. Photos will have short captions and are tagged to garnish attention.

That's what this site is all about. Photos, photos, and more photos.

If you are a budding photographer, then seriously look into this site. It could be a brilliant way to showcase your work for the world to see.

For writers, it's been suggested to use Instagram as a place to showcase flash fiction and short essays. You can use the photo as the first line in a story and use the caption to showoff your writing chops. This particular idea will take training of your followers, but some writers have used this idea to great effect.

And writers would benefit greatly from getting involved in the #Bookstagram community. It's filled with reviewers and those who are actively involved with books.

As a nice functionality to help in building your platform across multiple social media accounts, Instagram gives you the ability to cross-post your images to your Facebook profiles and pages, but exactly where those images go will depend on what type of Instagram account you have. At the time of writing this book, only *business* accounts could cross-post to public Facebook *pages*. All other accounts, including *creator* accounts (which is another type of *professional* account that you can access through Meta Business) cross-posts to your personal Facebook *profile*.

Biggest Risk Associated with Instagram

Instagram is connected to your Facebook accounts, even though they are different products. The *professional accounts* are connected and managed via the Meta Business tools. For some people, this could be an issue, as both Instagram and Facebook use the same core security features, and share some of the same tools (like Messenger).

THREADS

Threads is the new kid on the block, launching onto the scene in 2023. It is popular among the writing community, but finding the writing community can be difficult.

At the time of writing this book, Threads allowed for only one hashtag in posts, but hashtags didn't work in bios. Unless you knew exactly what hashtags to use on the platform, finding the community could be difficult. Most writers weren't using #writingcommunity.

Some writers have taken to using Threads to create essays filled with short segments that are linked together. Just hit the return button on a mobile device three times, and the next message in the threaded essay will automatically be created without posting the first one.

Biggest Risk Associated with Threads

The biggest issue with Threads is that your Threads account is tied to your Instagram account. If you decide to leave the site and delete your Threads account, you also delete your Instagram account. This is not something you want to do if you have carefully chosen your handles.

PINTEREST

If you are working on a book about crafts or a cookbook, then Pinterest might be the perfect site for you. Many of the users on Pinterest gather crafty ideas and other posts of that nature. However, the ability to share posts is limited; it's designed for sharing photos that link to other posts on the internet.

Do not fall into the trap of thinking that you could use Pinterest as a blogging site. That is not what it was designed for.

Biggest Risk Associated with Pinterest

Be careful with collaborative boards. You might have joined a collaboration to share pins with your joint audiences. But scammers are highly active on the site and have been known to hijack those collaborative boards.

Even if you leave the board, because you once collaborated on that board, your account is still linked to that board. Any negative repercussions that the board faces could also create negative repercussions for your account.

LINKEDIN

LinkedIn is a networking site for professionals such as engineers, businessmen, doctors, editors, etc. This is where professional freelance writers and editors can contact potential clients. However, you are unlikely to connect with the everyday reader.

While LinkedIn can help industry professionals link with other industry professionals, in my opinion, this site is not suitable for most writers.

Biggest Risk Associated with LinkedIn

For those using the site, there is a massive security issue within the default settings. The default settings on the site will share your contact details (email address and phone number, if you've included a phone number) with your full network. It may sound innocent until you discover what a *network* really is.

On LinkedIn, a *network* includes up to three degrees of separation from your direct *connections*.

Let's say that you have 5 connections, and let's say that each of those connections have 5 connections. And each of those connections have 5 connections. And each of those connections have 5 connections. If you were to do the math, that's 625 people who have access to your contact details by default.

In reality, most people have hundreds of connections.

SNAPCHAT

Snapchat is designed for teasers. Messages are sent to followers, then disappear after a short period of time.

The lack of longevity of posts means that followers might not see your message. Unless you intend to have fun with teasers, I would be leery of incorporating Snapchat into a writer's online platform.

Biggest Risk Associated with Snapchat

Ignoring issues with fake accounts, the app by default shares your location when you share your posts. In this day and age, this location sharing poses a massive security risk. Turn it off.

Open the app and go to your account settings, then scroll down until you find *Location*. Toggle *Ghost Mode* on.

REDDIT

Reddit is an American website designed for the distribution of social news and random web content. The biggest attraction of Reddit is the feature where one can ask random questions. This feature makes the site good for publicity directed towards the general public. In addition, there are writing communities where you can get advice about publishing, etc.

Exactly how this might work within your own platform—only you can answer that.

Biggest Risk Associated with Reddit

From a security perspective, Reddit seems to be one of the safest platforms out there. They take any security breach seriously, making public announcements of the breach within hours of it happening, and moving quickly to lock affected accounts (requiring users to log back in). And the number of breaches on record is small.

But you still need to check the site settings to ensure that you are using the settings that are best for you.

MASTODON

Mastodon became popular shortly after Elon Musk bought Twitter back in November 2022.

The Mastodon network itself is not a single server, but multiple servers spread throughout the world. All servers talk to one another if the right connections have been put in place.

Just find a server you like the name of and apply to join. Some servers use a vetting process, where you have to prove some detail about who you are. For example, to join *mastodon.nz*, you must be a New Zealand resident or have close ties to New Zealand. However, other servers, like *bookstodon.com*, are open until the server is full.

The site itself works much like X, where you post your message along with hashtags to get noticed. But unlike X, your feed is filled only with the hashtags and accounts you follow. There is no service curation of content.

So, new accounts will have an empty feed until you start following others and hashtags of interest. This makes the site great for building communities.

Biggest Risk Associated with Mastodon

Because Mastodon is not a centralized server, but rather made up of lots of servers, the security associated with Mastodon will be highly dependent on the server that you happen to be on.

Mastodon itself is an open-source project, meaning that anyone can download the program and start a server. But it also means that hackers are able to get the latest code and pull it to bits, hunting out the vulnerabilities in preparation for an attack. If server hosts don't have good security practices themselves, then everyone on that particular server is at risk. In the past, some servers have been hijacked by malicious hackers.

My recommendation for Mastodon users is to take advantage of the account forwarding features built into the system. Have accounts on multiple servers (I have accounts on *bookstodon.com* and *mastodon.nz*). Decide which account is your primary account, and have all other accounts forward to the main account. Should something happen to the server that you prefer to use, you have another account ready and waiting in the background. You switch the link forwarding to the other account, and off you go.

TikTok

If you like the idea of creating videos of yourself, then TikTok might be the site for you. The #BookTok community is strong and is where all the book reviewers hang out.

However, the site is Chinese owned, and has been restricted in some countries.

Biggest Risk Associated with TikTok

It turns out that TikTok has a limit on the number of times that you can "log out" and "log in" to the site. I don't know what the limit is, but whatever it is, I've reached it.

I was logging in to TikTok via the web browser on my computer. But every time you clear your cookies on your browser (which you should be doing on a regular basis), you are logged out of all sites, and you need to log in again.

Well . . . It turns out TikTok didn't like that. It took me in the order of two years to get back into my account again via a computer. I had been locked out—on any browser or any computer. I could still access the account via my phone, but the fact that I couldn't log out and log back in on a regular basis made me nervous. Hence, I personally don't use the site.

I don't know if the policies have changed, but in my opinion, the logout/login thing is a massive security flaw.

YOUTUBE

Most of us will use YouTube to find how-to videos or to check out the previews for that movie due to be released. But you will also find writing communities on YouTube that are connected to certain channels owned by writers and industry professionals.

If you are up for the challenge of creating informational videos (longer than the short things found on TikTok), then YouTube might be your playground of choice.

The nice thing about YouTube is that you can make videos subscriber only, where people need to subscribe to your newsletters to get the links for your content. I have a few newsletter subscriptions that make full use of this feature, answering subscriber questions on a weekly basis.

Biggest Risk Associated with YouTube

YouTube accounts are connected to your Google accounts. This is not necessarily a bad thing, but be aware that your security on YouTube is tied to your security on Google.

Just like everything else, ensure that you know what all of the settings do, and make sure that you are using the right settings for your situation.

And when Google suggests that you take a "security checkup", do it! They tend to send out those checkup notices every time there has been a change to one or more major security feature.

DISCORD

Discord is an odd beast, as it's not a discoverable social media site, not really. Networking happens in servers, and you need to get invited to join the party.

Different servers will employ different features and will be structured in different ways. Some servers make use of the audio and video chat features, while others make use of the forum features.

Many writer groups use Discord. The site has become a popular alternative to Facebook.

Discord embodies the idea of networking, and it's baked into the system design.

Biggest Risk Associated with Discord

On Discord, you have two different sets of security settings. You have your personal account settings, which include your 2FA features and whether people can send you private messages or not. But you also have your server settings.

The biggest risks on Discord are associated with the server settings. Unless you are the server admin, there's not a lot you can do about it.

Just ensure that you are using the right settings on your personal account settings and go from there.

SLACK

Slack is another system that is designed for networking only. Many businesses will use Slack to communicate with their teams.

Each Slack server is structured to suit the needs of the community using it. And you need to get invited to join the server. You can't find them any other way.

Biggest Risk Associated with Slack

The security on Slack is much like Discord, in that you have personal account settings and server security settings. Just do what you can about your personal account settings and go from there.

GRAVATAR

Gravatar is not a social media site, but the information in your Gravatar account is used to automatically add your name and profile photo to your comments when you add your thoughts to the bottom of that beloved blog post. (I bet you were wondering how the server got that information.)

If you have a WordPress account, then you will have a Gravatar account, though you might not know that it exists. But WordPress is not the only system that uses Gravatar to populate user profile information. Some of the older news sites use it too.

It is in your advantage to ensure that you have the right information loaded into the Gravatar system. Just because it looks all good from the WordPress end, doesn't mean that there isn't some information that you added to your Gravatar profile through another site; that information may now be in the public domain and you are completely unaware. The issue here is that editing your profile through WordPress, or the other site, will not necessarily edit your Gravatar profile.

To view your Gravatar profile, you need to visit *gravatar.com/Username/*, where *Username* is your WordPress user ID. From here, you can see exactly what is connected to your Gravatar profile.

Biggest Risk Associated with Gravatar

Be warned now: connecting Facebook to your Gravatar will connect your private profile, not your public page. If you want to link your public Facebook page, then you will need to add this as a separate website.

WHAT IS NOT SUITED FOR NETWORKING?

While there are many sites out there for making new connections and fostering working relationships, there are many sites and apps that are not intended for networking.

Any site or app designed for dating was never intended to advertise your writing. Do yourself a favor: don't go there.

And programs and apps like Skype, Google Meets, WhatsApp, and Messenger (from Meta, a.k.a. Facebook) are great tools for having private communications with people on the other side of the world. However, these apps were intended to foster connections that already exist. They were not designed to make new connections.

35

NEW ACCOUNTS

So, YOU'VE DECIDED THAT a particular social media site will be perfect for your needs. You've come up with a plan for producing content for the new account. And you're confident that it won't take away too much time from your other writer activities. Now, you're ready to sign up for that account and dive into this new world.

But it's not just a matter of posting messages. There are a few things you need to do when setting up those accounts.

YOUR CHOSEN HANDLE

Most systems allow you to choose your own handle. This will be a special *@name* that will help people to find you on the platform and link to your profiles. This user ID or handle is created at the time you create your account and is associated with your login information.

Back in chapter 11, we spoke about the importance of the right domain name in building your brand. Well, the same concepts apply to your social media accounts. You need to ensure whatever handle you choose will be identifiable and related to you, helping your fans to find you across all social media sites that you use.

I recommend that your standard handle be some variant of your pen name. If you have a long name, you might need to be clever in your handle selection, but if possible, I would try to keep it as close to your pen name as possible. If your chosen handle is already taken (which can happen), then play around with adding "writer" or "author" to your name.

On some sites (like X), you are able to change your handle without losing your followers. So, if you need to, you can re-purpose previous existing accounts. There is no need to create a new account if your old account already has a decent following.

Some writers will feel the urge to have multiple accounts on a given social media site, where each account services a different audience. There could be any number of strategic business reasons for why you might do this, but for every account you have, that's another account that you need to manage and be present on. Each new account still requires regular new content and engagement with followers. Avoid the trap of spreading yourself too thin.

Your Name

Every single account that I'm aware of gives you the ability to have a name listed that is different from your handle. Ideally, your chosen handle will be consistent across all social media sites. But even if you were forced to have different handles on different sites, your name doesn't change. So put in your name exactly how you would like to be identified.

Some writers and other industry professionals use their names to give additional information about what is happening in their little corner of the publishing industry.

. . . is working to a deadline

. . . —New release coming xDate

. . . (closed to queries)

Personally, I don't do this, because it can mess with your SEO and discoverability. Instead, I build that information into my bios.

THE BIO SECTION

Social media sites allow you to have a micro-bio listed. Yet, too many people leave the bios blank. And those blank bios are an instant turnoff for me.

When trying to decide if I'm going to follow someone on a given social media site or not, the first thing I do is look at their bios. I'm forgiving about a lot of things, but a blank bio will often result in an "ignore" response. In some situations, that blank bio results in a block. I have no way of knowing if the blank bio was an oversight or something more shady.

We went over how to craft the micro-bio back in chapter 13.

THE PROFILE PHOTO

We covered the nitty-gritty of profile photos back in chapter 12. Now it's time to put that profile photo to good use.

On every social media account you have, use the same image. This will help with the identification factor. If, for whatever reason, you were unable to get your chosen handle, people could still identify your account by the familiar profile image.

THE COVER PHOTO

The cover photo is the image that goes across the top of your profile page. This is your place to showcase your book covers or whatever images that resonate with your brand and writing.

The size of the cover photo is different for every site, so you might need to carefully construct a new cover photo for each social media account.

Keep in mind that most people won't see your cover image unless they visit your profile. Your profile image, on the other hand, is shown every time you interact with some content on the site.

LINKS TO YOUR WEBSITE

Most social media sites give you the ability to add a link to an external site. My recommendation is to use your website.

Some writers use Linktree or something similar, but I'm always thinking about SEO. The more traffic you can drive back to your website, the better off you are. Everything you might link to a Linktree profile should be listed on your website.

PUBLIC OR PRIVATE

On many social media sites, you can specify if your account is public (where anyone can see your posts, even if they don't follow you) or private (where you get the opportunity to vet everyone who asks to follow you).

For teenager accounts, ones who are not celebrity figures, I recommend private accounts. This gives the teen more control over their followers, and they can screen out the creepy dudes. But for writers and other public figures, a private account kind-of defeats the purpose of why you have the account—to get found.

(A side note: Most social media sites will not let users under the age of 18 have a public account.)

Here's something to consider: When I get a new follower on any of my social media accounts, I often look at who followed me and decide if I would like to follow back—if I would like to network with that person. If the account is private, and I don't know the person from somewhere else, it's a no-follow from me. I need to be able to see if the posts are the sorts of things that I'm going to happily interact with.

Building a Following by Following Accounts

One of the best ways to build your network is to start following accounts and to start interacting. Comment and reply. Start building those connections. And if someone follows you, take the time to decide if you want to follow them in return.

I don't subscribe to the "follow back" philosophy. I don't follow everyone who follows me, and I don't expect everyone who I follow to follow me in return. For me, it's about building connections.

When trying to decide whether I'll follow an account or not, I ask myself the following questions.

Is the profile just an ad reel?

If it's nothing but "Buy my book", it's likely to be a "No thanks" from me.

Does the person share their own opinions? Inspirational quotes are cool, but how many of them are there?

Some of those quotes are brilliant nuggets of truths, but I tend to follow those who express their own thoughts and feelings on occasion.

Are the posts being shared from another social media site? Is the account holder active and present on this site?

Remember, it's about being social and interacting with others. Don't rely so much on automation that you look like a bot.

Does the subject of the posts and messages interest me?

In reality, if your feed is just plain fascinating, I won't care how many links you include, or whether the feed is clearly automated. I'll follow you anyway.

THE FIRST POST AND PINNED POSTS

If you are new to the site, then that first post will be your chance to make a good first impression. Introduce yourself and invite others to interact with you.

On occasion, you will post something that you want people who visit your profile to see. Turn these into pinned posts, i.e., messages pinned to the top of your profile.

Not all sites have the pinned posts feature, and some sites allow for more than one pinned post. Take advantage of those pinned posts to showcase your latest release or some important news.

HASHTAG USAGE

Most of the popular social media sites allow for the use of hashtags to improve searchability for your posts and messages. Hashtags are often connected to certain factions of the community.

For example: #Bookstagram is the book reviewers' hashtag on Instagram, where #Booktok is where the book reviewers hang out on TikTok. You will find #WritingCommunity on X, Mastodon, and Instagram, but #MSWL seems to be only on X.

As you start to dive deeper and deeper into your new social media site, you will learn which hashtags are needed to reach your chosen community. However, don't go overboard with the hashtag thing. Too many hashtags could result in the same negative reception that no hashtags can.

REMEMBER SITE SETTINGS

If you haven't already gone through the site settings with a fine-tooth comb, it's important that you do so before the account becomes too widely spread. Make sure that you know exactly what every setting does and that you are using the right settings for your circumstances.

Site settings are part of basic internet security.

And remember to set up those two-factor authentication systems if you have access to them. Protect your accounts the best you can.

GET A FRIEND TO CHECK IT

Once you have everything set up, get a trusted friend to look over your account from their end. Get them to look over it and make sure that you aren't inadvertently leaking information. Or that you aren't doing anything that makes you look like a dweeb.

All systems have their flaws, and sometimes you could be leaking information without knowing it.

HAVE FUN WITH THE ACCOUNT!

Social media can be a chore, but if you have fun with what you are doing, you'll make it fun for yourself and your followers.

So, now that your new account has been set up, it's time to get to work and start networking.

36

ONE WRONG WORD IS ALL IT TAKES

ON MY PERSONAL BLOG, I often play the bad-guy card, looking at how a creepy stalker dude or hacker can take what we post and turn it against us. I write thrillers, so diving into the head of creepy bad guy is something that I do on a regular basis. It is through the bad-guy persona that I'm able to highlight how certain activities are dangerous.

However, there is another danger out there that doesn't come from people who are intent on doing us harm. Sometimes, the harm comes from those who have good intentions, but they still cut us deeply.

As writers, we carefully craft our sentences to use the perfect word to say what we want to say. There are times when we spend days trying to find those perfect words. Yet, there is one aspect of our writing lives where many writers don't take the same care with words as they do their stories.

I'm talking about posts on social media.

The rush to get the post out there can sometimes land us in situations where words cut like knives.

We could be writing what we thought was inspirational and encouraging. But one word misinterpreted could shift the entire tone of the message to something that many take as negative and demeaning.

I've seen it happen.

In one of my many discussion groups on Facebook, a friend posted what was meant to be an inspirational post about writers never giving up. But one word left this tone of attack towards those who were self-publishing. The resulting comments were a barrage of attacks that focused on the one word and not the overall message. The writer of the post, whom I had personal contact with, broke down. She didn't realize how one word could cause such a negative experience.

Time to put on the psychology hat for a moment.

PEOPLE FOCUS ON THE NEGATIVE

No matter how positive a message is, people focus on the negative.

It's human nature to look at the world through negative eyes. We commonly shy away from praise, and we're so quick to go for the jugular when someone does something that we don't like. Add into this volatile mix the power that words really have, and the writers are the first to be lynched.

Writers on social media need to take extra care when constructing messages, especially ones that are meant to be motivational and inspirational.

The issue stems from the fact that humor doesn't translate to the written word, not when it's out of context.

Within a book, writers can take the time to build the setting, to show the character's wit and sarcasm. Those carefully chosen words build the picture in the reader's mind. When the humor occurs in those written passages, the reader is laughing, because they can visualize the entire scenario.

On social media, we're writing as a hybrid character that is built from components of ourselves. In person, a writer might be the most gentle, loving, and hilarious person; however, online, the words chosen could give the impression that you're an insensitive, sadistic monster.

It's not a simple matter of crafting messages with correct grammar and punctuation. Sometimes, it's a single word that can change the entire tone of a sentence.

TONE AND INTENT DO NOT ALWAYS TRANSLATE

Take the following example:

> *No man has a good enough memory to be a successful liar.*

Without the context, that line can mean different things. It can be interpreted as negative and cruel, accusing a person of shady deals. Or it could be a reminder how we need to be truthful and honest, because no one has the memory needed to remember all the lies told in a lifetime.

However, when Abraham Lincoln spoke those famous words, he was talking about how one needs to have trust from those around him to be successful.

Let's consider another example where a single word can change the entire meaning of a sentence:

> *It was hard for Eric to accept the punishment for his deeds.*

Compare that with:

> *It was hard for Eric to accept the just punishment for his deeds.*

It's only one word, but that one word changes the tone of the writing.

Writers are skilled at this level of wordplay. We train and spend painstaking hours to finely hone that ability.

We need to use that ability on social media too.

Reread Your Posts Before You Hit Send

Today's society is in a rush. Every thought is tapped out onto a smartphone and posted to our various social media accounts without much thought. The send button is selected before we know it. However, there is a joke among writers and editors: The best copyediting happens *after* we hit the send button.

Some years ago, I wrote an article on my personal blog about how the autocorrect beast was constantly getting the better of me. My most famous autocorrect moment was when I asked a friend if she could babysit for me. However, my phone decided that I didn't need a *babysitter.* According to my phone, I needed a *babyshitter.* My girlfriend and I laugh to this day about that one. But it's a living reminder of how important it is to read and reread every message that goes out before I hit send (and even then, the odd hilarity slips through).

Before hitting send, take an extra 10 seconds to reread your post to ensure that you haven't said something that you would come to regret later. In my mind, it's 10 seconds well spent.

I'm not suggesting that you spend a full day to carefully construct that tweet of 280 characters, unless, of course, you want to spend a full day on that tweet. If you're constructing an elevator pitch for your latest book, I can see the desire to spend not one day constructing that tweet but multiple days. However, always look at your posts and tweets with the brush of another's eyes.

Do You Care How Another Reacts?

For every post you send out, ask yourself the following questions:

1) Will this post come across as funny like you had intended?
2) Or will it be insulting?
3) Do you care either way?

I'm dead serious about this one, folks. It's social media. You're going to ruffle feathers along the way. Not everyone thinks the way you do. Just like your stories won't appeal to everyone, neither will your social media posts.

I have posted comments on social media that rubbed people up the wrong way myself, but they were meant to. They were designed to get people thinking. And I got the responses I expected, including personal attacks. However, I was able to ignore those attacks, simply because when I posted those messages, I didn't care if I was attacked for them. I knew there were enough people out there who would see things from my perspective that it was worth the risk.

Don't aim for perfection—aim for something that you can be proud of. This goes for everything in life, folks, including your social media.

37

INTERACTIONS VIA PRIVATE COMMUNICATIONS

PRIVATE COMMUNICATIONS OR DIRECT messaging systems are part of the social media equation. Not every interaction you have will be out in the open for everyone to see.

Perhaps you are arranging to exchange manuscripts with a new beta reader. You want that email address exchange to be behind the scenes in private. (Well, as private as anything on the internet can be.) But depending on the settings involved with your systems, private messages can come from anywhere.

The majority of my social media accounts are dedicated to the author/writer/editor. Some of my clients find me via social media. I allow direct messages to my private social media accounts for this reason—but communications regarding editing contracts are quickly moved to email and off of social media, so I can easily maintain a record of communications for legal purposes.

But when those friendship scams come knocking . . . It's called *block*.

Here are some general rules that I follow when trying to decide whether I'll entertain that conversation that comes in via direct messages.

In the initial communication, is there any indication as to where I might know that person from? How did the conversation start?

Sometimes, the conversation starts with an interaction in a writing group or the like. If I recognize the name and the profile image from the Facebook group, or whatever group I was in at the time, then all is good. I'll happily respond, and off I go.

Sometimes, the communication comes from another lead, but normally the initial message includes something that explains how the person heard about me or how I might know them. I met them at a conference. Or maybe a writing friend suggested that they reach out to me. Or maybe they were doing a Google search and my name came up as somebody who might be able to help them with their writing.

There are a lot of different reasons why someone might want to contact me. The point is there is normally a reason mentioned.

If I'm the one initializing the conversation, which I have been known to do, I always include how I first interacted with that person in any direct message or email communication. Even when I send cold emails to people, you will always find a reason for why the communication is happening.

On social media, is the account involved a private account?

On Instagram, if the communication is coming from a private account, I tend to just ignore it, unless it has met the criteria from the first point. I don't want to spend my time interacting with someone who has a private account without a good reason to be doing so. I want to be able to see what sorts of things a person shares online. I want to see what their brand is about.

I have the same policy on X and Mastodon.

Facebook is an abnormality, but my interactions on Facebook are not 100% professional. I have personal and family interactions on Facebook too.

Are the Spidey senses going off?

This is a bit harder to explain, but I have a natural instinct about people. I can tell when someone is going to be problematic. I can tell when someone is going to be a bit shady. And I can tell when someone is being honest but doesn't understand the technology.

This is not something that I can easily show you how to develop. It's about understanding human nature and the way people commonly behave given a certain set of circumstances.

I have rarely been wrong about someone's motivations in their interactions. This instinct has saved my life more times than I care to count, so I just trust it.

In the next few chapters, we'll be taking a dive into how things can go horribly wrong on the internet and how to deal with things like cyberbullying. But for the most part, learn to trust your instincts. If you are feeling uncomfortable with any interaction online, there will be a reason for it, even if you don't fully understand that reason.

PART SEVEN

WHEN THE INTERNET GOES WRONG

38

NOTHING IS PRIVATE ON THE INTERNET

MOST EMPLOYERS MONITOR THEIR employee's emails for anything that could have a negative backlash on the company. They monitor for spamming and abusive language. They monitor for inappropriate communications. This is standard practice, particularly in government agencies and high-profile companies. And it's for this reason that many people will use personal accounts for certain activities.

But if cops can be fired because of comments made on a private Twitter account when they were teenagers, it's foolish to think that anything that goes through the internet can't come back and bite you in the ass.

It has happened multiple times over the years when so-called private communications were made public because of a screen capture.

DO YOU REMEMBER COCKYGATE?

If you look back to 2018—or for that matter, just type CockyGate into your favored search engine and see what comes up—you'll encounter a trademark scandal that swept through the publishing industry. No corner of the industry was safe from the backlash.

Most of the articles published at the time centered on the trademark mess that happened. But there were other lessons to be learned about what happened too, lessons about the hidden traps of the internet.

In 2018, I wrote two different articles about some of the lessons to be learned from the situation. On my personal blog, I focused on the mob mentality of those attacking *all* trademarks being lodged, including the legitimate ones, and how people were being bullied in the extreme. On the Black Wolf Editor's Blog, I commented on how having a drunken rant on Facebook Live was probably the worst thing that an author (or any public figure) could do, and again I spoke about mob mentality on social media.

But there was a hidden trap that even I had overlooked. Looking back on it now, it was so obvious.

CockyGate started because someone took a screen capture of an email and shared it on Twitter (now known as X). What was intended as private communications was made public.

But if CockyGate is not enough of a scandal for you, there was also the email that was made public, dismissing a member of the ethics committee for Romance Writers of America in 2019. That email communication wasn't even shared publicly by the person who received the email but rather by the writer's friend.

And in November, 2021, another scandal erupted when Victoria Strauss released a blog post on the Writer Beware blog about an editor and their shady practices. [1] Within the editors' circles, there was concern about this particular editor's practices and how it might reflect on editors as a whole, but most of the conversations I saw centered around the shocking nature of the editor's emails and communications.

I don't want to get into the disconnect between client expectations and services provided by this editor, because that's not the hidden trap I want to highlight. I want to focus entirely on the fact that the whole world now knows exactly how that editor communicates. And the reason we now know this is because a screen capture of email communications was shared as part of the Writer Beware blog post.

That is the hidden trap.

(A link to the Writer Beware blog post is found at the end of this chapter.)

IT'S KNOWN AS BEING DISCOVERABLE

Above, I commented on how it's common practice for businesses and government agencies to monitor email communications of their employees. This is because if anything should happen where legal action is being pursued, the lawyers involved could request those email communications. At that point, even that secret recipe for Grandma Tilly's cookies could become subject to scrutiny.

Just because those emails are electronic doesn't mean that there isn't a "paper trail" of the communications. And taking a screen capture of that communication adds another layer of complexity to the discoverability factor.

But let's shift this conversation completely away from emails and talk about something that some people might not consider as discoverable.

EVEN PRIVATE CHATS ARE NOT PRIVATE

Prior to 2023, I took part in a daily morning write-in on a chat room facility that I and a small group of writers had been using for years. The room was a public room, and anyone could join in. Sometimes, you would get the odd creepy dude coming into the room that started using the private chat facilities for one-on-one conversations, making the others in the room uncomfortable.

There was one morning where we had someone go into the room claiming to be a psychologist wanting to talk about his patient. The ethical gray area here was part of the concern that most of us in the room had. On the surface, what he was doing seemed innocent enough, until he started sending "private" messages to each of us in turn, cornering us in his odd conversation. What the guy didn't know was that each user was taking screen captures of the conversations and sharing them with the moderators for the room.

That's how I got involved.

I could see how the conversations made each of the room users feel uncomfortable. It wasn't any one particular statement, but the sum of the conversation. And when he cornered me with his "private" chat . . .

He was mortified to learn that his so-called "private" chats were actually public knowledge. Me, being me, explained to him how nothing on the internet is private. I told him about the screen captures of the conversations, and he never came back.

I don't know if his reasons for being in the room with a group of writers were legitimate or not, but he learned a lesson about one of the most dangerous hidden traps associated with the internet—or at least I hoped he learned it.

It doesn't matter what the channel is. Nothing is private on the internet. Not emails. Not personal messages. Not even chat room conversations.

THE LESSONS I TAUGHT MY CHILDREN

The world of social media is here to stay. My children have never known any differently. Because of who I am, I've made sure my children know exactly what sort of dangers exist on the internet.

It has been said again and again in this house that you never say or do anything on the internet that you wouldn't be happy with if it was ever made public. It doesn't matter how "private" something professes to be. There will always be loopholes in the system and some information could easily get leaked. And if you ever make it big (delusions of grandeur are allowed), there will be people out there looking for the dirt . . . and they will find it. Don't make it easy for them.

When I see articles showing screen captures of private communications, I make sure that my children at least know about it, because nothing is private on the internet.

(And yes, I have become a broken record.)

My children are highly conversant on how easy it is to take a screen capture on their own phones—a little feature that my daughter took advantage of when a bully decided to use Snapchat to attack her, resulting in disciplinary actions taken by her high school against the other student involved. Snapchat is designed so the messages disappear after they've been seen, but screen captures are there for as long as you need them.

That's the point.

This little hidden trap will happily catch out the bullies and the idiots, because they falsely believe that private communications will remain private. Meanwhile, the rest of us who are a little tech savvy will take a screen capture of that abusive message. And if the ones attacking us continue to be abusive . . .

Well, I think you get the moral of this story.

WRITER BEWARE AND VICTORIA STRAUSS

If you are new to the publishing industry, then you will want to check out the Writer Beware blog (writerbeware.blog). It is sponsored by *Science Fiction and Fantasy Writers of America, Inc.* The entire blog is dedicated to highlighting the scams and charlatans that might prey on the unsuspecting writer.

Sometimes, it's a dodgy publisher or shamgent (a shady so-called agent). Other times, it's contract clauses that are deeply concerning and open up a writer to a world of hurt. And other times, it's just keeping the writing world up to date with the crazy that is known as #DisneyMustPay.

The blog posts on the site use screen captures, which contain the information that the post is warning us against. I would avoid using a reader that strips the images from the posts. Those images _are_ the post.

The posts are not about tearing people down, but rather ensuring that writers know about the dangers that exist, so we are able to traverse the muddy waters of the publishing industry a little more safely.

While this book is about the hidden traps of the internet, Writer Beware is about the hidden traps of the publishing industry.

REFERENCES FOR THIS CHAPTER

[1] Victoria Strauss (November 21, 2021) *An Editing Nightmare: Editor and Author Coach Christina Kaye of Book Boss Academy (Formerly Write Your Best Book).* Writer Beware. https://writerbeware.blog/2021/11/12/an-editing-nightmare-editor-and-author-coach-christina-kaye-of-write-your-best-book-aka-book-boss-academy

39

HIDDEN SECURITY RISKS IN PHOTOS AND VIDEOS

BECAUSE OF THE EVOLUTION of smartphones, so many of us now carry a high-resolution camera in our back pockets (or in my case, the outside pocket of my purse). It's not surprising that people are becoming shutter bugs. With smartphones having easy access to the internet, many people want to post those photos to show off their latest escapades. Now that the technology has progressed into the world of video and live streaming . . .

Smartphones have transformed our world in ways that come right out of science fiction. But with this newfound freedom comes a level of responsibility that many people ignore.

At this point, I'm going to ignore the instances where terrorists have streamed their nightmare acts to Facebook, or where teens decided to share their pet cruelty criminal behavior on YouTube. (And both of these acts happened within New Zealand.) Sharing your criminal activities on any social media is like painting a target on your forehead and begging the cops to come and arrest you—because that is exactly what will happen.

Thankfully, most users of social media are not terrorists or criminals, but what about the drunken frat parties that get filmed and posted? At the time, your comments might seem funny. They might even seem innocent. But people have lost their jobs over such lapses in judgment.

I remember quite clearly the news articles about a couple's after-hours sexual escapades in the office that were caught on smartphones from patrons at the bar across the street.

These are all extreme examples that most people are not going to encounter, but sometimes the everyday mundane things could be just as dangerous when shared on social media.

We have already covered most of the ideas in this chapter earlier in this book, but we're going to go over them again because they are that important.

HIDDEN PRIVATE DETAILS

Consider the example of the new car. Seems innocent enough. Let's face it, getting a new car is a big deal, and you want to share that joy with all your friends. Take a few pictures of how pretty that car is, and share them on social media.

WAIT! Before you hit the share button, take a good look at that photo.

Is the license plate number showing in that photo? In many countries, car registration records can be easily obtained by the public. Refer back to chapter 6 for more information on this.

Here is another example of something seemingly innocent. Outdoor Christmas decorations. To get the full effect, you need to get the whole house in that photo or video. And in the middle is your house number on the mailbox, and parked in the driveway is your car with its hi-vis license plate. And there's a random comment about what street you might live on somewhere else on your feed. With your unique display, and the photos whizzing through the internet to unknown corners of the world, anyone can work out the right time to rob you blind.

As part of research for one of my manuscripts, I was able to get the street address and full interior photos of a holiday home in Oregon with little to no effort. All the information I needed to let my fingers do the walking was present in the photos of the holiday home listing. So much for not having the address unless you made a booking.

But let's think about another scenario, one that many writers would likely post themselves. Unboxing the print version of your books.

Let's face it, those covers are so beautiful and we need to share them with the world. We get the knife out to cut the tape on the box and take a video of us doing the whole unveiling process. But where is the address label on that box?

And remember about the metadata of those images too. Thankfully, the more common social media sites will strip the metadata as you upload the photos, but if you need a little reminder about this particular danger, go back and reread *Chapter 26: Working with Images*.

EDIT PHOTOS AND VIDEOS FOR THE SECURITY DETAILS

If you are going to actively share photos or videos on social media, no matter the subject, learn how to use the editing tools that come on your smartphone or invest in editing software. Vet every image carefully. Ensure that there is nothing in that photo you wouldn't feel comfortable with if it was shared with the world.

And if you see your friends posting information that shouldn't go out, tell them. They might not know that they've done it.

THE GOLDEN SECURITY RULE OF SOCIAL MEDIA

When it comes to anything to do with social media (and the internet as a whole), it doesn't matter how *private* something professes to be, there will always be loopholes in the system and some information will get leaked.

Never put anything on any form of social media that you wouldn't feel comfortable with if it was ever made public.

Trust me, if you ever make it big, there will be people out there looking for dirt, and they will find it. Don't make it easy for them.

40
SCAMMERS

IN BUILDING OUR ONLINE platforms, we need to interact with others. Otherwise, what is the point? The purpose of a platform is to network. But when it comes to our interactions with strangers, we still need to keep our wits about us.

It's time for me to put on my bad-guy persona and give you some insights into how the more shady characters of the internet really go about their business, conning you out of . . . Well, not just your money, but your pride and your self-esteem.

ONLINE FRIENDSHIP SCAMS

We, as humans, tend to be trusting by nature. We want to think the best of people. Even after we've had that trust violated, we still want to think that people, for the most part, are good people—and most people are good people. But there is something about social media and the internet that seems to attract the shady parts of society.

Our gut instincts about an interaction might be telling us that something is off. Yet, so many people (and not just women) fall prey every day to the friendship scams. If you don't believe me, just boot up Netflix and bring up the documentary series on the *Tinder Swindler,* or the series *Inventing Anna*, or any other series that is about the underhanded deeds of con artists.

Con artists are good at spotting the trusting souls they can take advantage of. And it's because of our innate trusting nature that we don't want to think ill of people. So, we let the con artist con us.

But we can stop the con in its tracks by taking a few simple steps to protect ourselves—particularly when the con starts with a smarmy email or message about how pretty we are.

Every day, I seem to get some creepy dude trying to connect with me through one of my various social media accounts, telling me how pretty I look. Those messages are filled with flattery—sugary sweet compliments that almost make me want to hurl. But remember, I'm not your typical internet user either.

Those flattery messages are how online friendship scams start. They prey on those who might feel down about themselves. The scammers might comment on your smile. Maybe they comment on the photos you share. With every interaction, they're trying to break down the tough exterior you might have and get under your skin . . . so you trust them.

I got one the other day that started with "I got your name from one of your friends," but the message quickly descended in trying to sell me something.

Block!

A writer-specific variant of the online friendship scam might start with someone who seems to be taking an interest in your writing. So, you exchange a few messages, but the conversation quickly turns to them wanting to sell you something, or promising you publication, or getting that best-selling ranking if only you would spend money.

Block!

Then you get the odd interaction that is perfectly innocent to start. As the interactions carry on, questions start to form in your head. Is the person on the other end genuine? Are they even human?

When it comes to any of your interactions online, particularly on social media, you need to trust your instincts. If something feels off, then it's off. Simple as that. You don't need to identify the source of those feelings. Just accept that they're there and move on.

And block the offending accounts.

Texting Scams

One of the most common scams in New Zealand is a texting scam sent to people that says:

> *hey mom my phones broken I need some money to buy new phone*

The text message even contains the bad grammar that is commonly used in texting language by the younger generation.

If you're a parent of a teenager, receiving a message like the one above is not something out of the realm of possibility. Back in 2021, my daughter texted me saying that her phone was dying and that she needed a new phone. My instant response was that we could discuss it when she got home from school. When she got home, she showed me the most spectacular screen problem she had. Her entire screen was nothing but purple, and you had zero chance of seeing what was under that purple. Yeah, she needed a new phone.

But my daughter had learned years ago that I'm not going to be an instant "yes" for anything. If she caught me when I was in "work" mode, which was the most likely state she would catch me while she was at school, she could almost guarantee that I would respond to any of her text messages with something like "No, I'm working. Bugger off." I love my daughter, but I get grumpy when I'm hyper-focused.

But the "help me mom" scams have another layer to them. A parent believes the text messages and is prepared to send their children money. They then receive a text message with a specific bank account number to deposit the money into. This won't be a bank account number that the parent has seen before, but the con artist on the other end of the line has a plausible reason for the new account number lined up and ready to go.

The victims of this particular text scam are trusting and want to believe in the good in people. So, they pay the money without doing additional checks—and get stung.

But the text-based scams are not restricted to just the "help me mom" variant. Writing buddies of mine have gotten text messages saying that their packages have been held up at customs, and that they have to click the link to release the package—and pay money.

With the amount of packages that authors seem to get, particularly in my local area, it's not surprising how many people have been caught unaware by these scams.

The easiest way to avoid a text-based scam is to *go back to the source* from which it looks like the messages are coming from.

For the texting scams that look like they come from your children . . . Well, you need to go back to your children.

For those scams that look like they come from a courier delivering your packages, go back to the companies that sent you those packages and check the tracking numbers. And if you need to, get a person on the phone.

And if the texter gets persistent, block the offending number.

Login Scams (Also Known as "Contact Us" Scams)

Sometimes, I get an email that on the surface looks legit, telling me that there was a problem with my account, and that I need to login to correct the issue. In these emails, there will often be a button or link to click, taking me to a website that also looks legit. The unsuspecting user would then enter their login details . . . and the annoying scammer now has your username and password for whatever system they wanted access to.

My husband fell prey to this exact type of scam back in 2022. It was an email that looked like it came from work, telling him that he needed to login to the system to correct an issue. He clicked the link, logged in using his work credentials, did whatever the system wanted him to do, and didn't think anything else of it . . . until he got a phone call from the IT guys at his work, asking him if he just tried to log in from Germany. Yeah, my husband was the trusting soul who fell prey to an email login scam.

The IT guys quickly reset his systems and forced him to create new passwords. And it was a lesson learned the hard way: Don't click random links in emails! Thankfully, no harm was done, other than my husband gaining a bruised ego.

(He was incredibly sheepish as he told me what had happened. "And no doubt, I'll be your next blog post," he said. And yes, he was, but I love him just the same.)

If the login scams came in via email only, it would be easy to deal with them by using our spam filters. However, I get login scams via social media too.

They commonly come in via direct messages, which again is easy to manage by specifying who can and can't send direct messages. But it's the "tagging" posts that were new to me until I encounter my first one of those in early 2023.

The settings for my public Facebook page allow people to send me direct messages and tag my page. I do this for marketing reasons. I know the risks, and I accept those risks.

The original intention for the tagging was to allow my readers to show off anything that they might get from me they thought was awesome, adding a link to their posts that automatically linked back to my Facebook page. But I also have my system set up to send me a notification whenever anyone tags my public page in a post. This is so I know exactly what my name is being associated with. (There are settings within Facebook that allow me to remove my page or profile from tagged posts . . . and I have used them.)

So, when I got a notification saying that some random page I had never heard of before tagged me, I clicked on the notification. It took me to a post that said the following:

> *We need to re-verify the admin account's profile on all*
> *currently promoted pages*
> *This may result in some features on your page being*
> *restricted. Click the link below to verify.*
> *<<insert dodgy link>>*
> *You will need to verify your account to get back to normal.*
> *If you do not verify, we may permanently disable your*
> *account and page*
> *To ensure the rights of users, all users must comply with out*
> *policy*
> *Thank you for reading this message*

The above message was followed by an insane number of bullets and empty lines, then a list of 30+ tagged accounts, and my public page just happened to be one of them.

Okay . . . There are so many things wrong with this scenario that it screamed out, "Scam!"

1) Facebook would *never* use a random third party to highlight issues with pages.
2) Facebook would *never* send a public post tagging pages for something like this. They would send a notification that was for my eyes only.
3) The link in question was an HTTP URL that was made up of a long series of numbers. HTTP protocols went out the window years ago, and my web browser gets super pissy whenever I visit any website that hasn't updated to HTTPS protocols. And any website URL that is made up of a series of random numbers . . . Um . . . Dude, not clicking! (And no, I didn't need to click the link to get that information. It was directly written in the post. I didn't include it above, because I didn't want someone clicking on a dodgy link by mistake.)
4) Did you notice the lack of punctuation in the above quoted message? Because that is a sure-fire sign that it was written by someone who doesn't understand business

English. Again, this is not something that would happen to this extent from an official Facebook message. (The official messages from Facebook still have grammatical issues, but not the blatant lack of punctuation.) Now, I will grant you that with the introduction of ChatGPT, messages like the one above would be a lot cleaner, but you can still spot them as scams, because of the biggest reason . . .

5) I never signed up for any service that promotes my page. I don't even use Facebook ads. Does that tell you something?

It was alarm bells from start to finish. But clearly, there was something within the message that triggered something else.

Because it's me, I took a screen capture of the original offending message and wrote a "public service announcement" post on my public Facebook page . . . and I suddenly got inundated by all these comments containing links to people who could "help unlock my account." I lost track of how many of those comments came in.

I responded to the first ones, believing they were legit people trying to be helpful, but after fifteen or so comments of that nature within two minutes, I turned off the comments for that post and deleted the comments.

Then I got bombarded by private messages with the links, stating that I needed to respond to them.

I think I generated in the order of 4 or 5 separate posts on my public Facebook feed about the nightmare that ensued. I was laughing at the hilarity of the situation as I was writing them, but OMG . . . What a headache to manage on a Saturday morning. There were definitely lessons learned from the incident.

The biggest lesson was how all posts on your Facebook page by default will allow anyone to comment on your posts, even those who don't follow you. However, you can change those settings for individual posts, restricting comments to established followers only (i.e., accounts that have been following my page for more than 24 hours). I just wish that Facebook would allow this to be a generic setting for your page, but nope . . . it seems to be post dependent.

How Wide Spread is Your Email Address?

With all the email-based scams that come in, most of them being of the login scam variety, I always laugh at how badly worded those emails are, trying to sound official. Whoever wrote them really had no clue about how English grammar works.

I mean, they could at least learn how to use MS Word's grammar checker. I know it's not the best, but it would deal with the lack of capitalization.

While I can spot a scam a mile away, there will be many unsuspecting people out there who will be gullible enough to fall for the scam. It may be only one in 10,000 people, but it's statistically significant enough for scammers to keep doing it.

And a scammer's favorite playground is email. Far too many people get emails and blindly click on the links without understanding what they're clicking on.

Of course, the first question that many people ask is how did the scammer get your email in the first place? Well, let me tell you exactly how they got it.

Leaking Emails via Social Media

To have a social media account, you have to have an email address. But on most social media sites, there is a setting that will determine whether your email address is publicly available or not.

On Facebook, there's a setting that determines whether people can find you through your email or phone number—a bit like an old-fashioned phone book. By default, new accounts have this setting turned on.

On LinkedIn, contact details (emails and phone numbers) are made public within your network by default. And on LinkedIn, a *network* is up to three degrees of separation from your *connections*. If we did the math based on five connections for users, there are 625 people who have access to your contact details through LinkedIn. But of course, most users of the site have hundreds of connections. That is a lot of people who have access to your email address and phone number by default.

Other social media sites are just as "leaky".

Membership sites often have a setting somewhere that will make your email address public or private. But even if you have your email set to private, that might not mean that your email is "private" private. For some of my memberships, that setting specifies if my email address is shared on my member profile, which is accessible by the public. Members can still get my email via other means, including the "reply in private" feature available in the forums site used by the organization.

There is a reason I keep telling you to look at your account settings and make sure you know what they do.

So, getting email addresses off of social media and networking sites is easy, if you know what you're looking for.

But the scammers also get your emails from your websites.

SCRAPER BOTS

Scraper bots are automated programs that go through an entire website and pull out every email address listed on that site. That includes email addresses hidden behind contact forms.

It has gotten to the point that if you use a contact form and you haven't used CAPTCHA or something similar, the email address attached to those contact forms can quickly be overloaded with spam.

But that doesn't stop the scammers. As long as they can scrape your email address, you can be scammed via email.

Many scams that find my inbox involve an email address that a scrapper bot got from one of my websites. And I know that the scams came from scrapper bots because on my websites, I use special *public-facing communications email addresses* that are only found on my websites.

When an email comes in via my website (and via the special website-only email), I respond from a different email address, leaving that public-facing communications email for the bots. I do this to protect my accounts.

And if that special email address gets overrun by spam, it's a simple matter to change it out for another one, creating a new sacrificial lamb for the scrapper bots.

Avoiding Email-based Scams

With the number of scams that come in via email, there are a few things that you can do to protect yourself.

Use a Spam Filter

The simplest way to avoid many email-based scams is to use a spam filter. Most email servers have one built in.

If you want, you can turn the settings up, so the spam filters become aggressive and block everything, but aggressive filters often make more work than they're worth. (And any prospective clients who uses aggressive spam filters quickly gets dumped into the "don't bother" category. I have better things to do with my time than to fool the spam filter into letting my communications through.)

Within my own practice, I tend to leave the spam filters alone with whatever settings they want to use. Spam emails still get through, and even on their current settings, the spam filters often capture emails that aren't spam, but they block the worst of the spam and scam offenders. I make a habit of checking my spam folders once a month, just in case something got captured that wasn't meant to be captured.

Don't Trust Links

It might seem obvious, but no matter what, don't trust the links in an email from a source that you don't know. Even if the email looks legit, don't click the links in the email. Just don't.

Instead, go to the website yourself and log in that way.

> Always go back to the source.

Interesting fact: Whenever I get a message from my bank or from the IRD (the tax department in New Zealand), the notification will say that there is a message waiting for me and that I need to login to find the message. But there is never a link to log on. It is assumed that I know what the web address is for the login page. (And this is just one of the ways that I know that any emails that look like they come from my bank or from the IRD are frauds. Because the real emails never contain links.)

Use Two-Factor Authentication (2FA)

For every system possible, especially your banking system or anything else that is connected to your money, use 2FA. It's surprising the number of hackers that could have been stopped in their tracks if people would just use 2FA.

(We went over 2FA systems in chapter 3.)

Blacklist the Offending Sender Email

If the offending sender email or domain gets annoying, constantly sending you "login" scam emails, then blacklist the email or domain. Block them.

By blacklisting an email address, you're telling your spam filter that, no matter what, it's to send all emails from that address directly to the spam folder. Eventually, you'll need to clean out your spam folder, but at least they won't be taking up space in your inbox.

Blacklisting has another impact that people might not be aware of. If enough people blacklist an email address, then email servers like Gmail will flag the entire offending domain as spam and send those emails to the spam folder for *all* email users, including those who haven't blacklisted the offending email address. It doesn't stop the persistent scammer from getting a new email address, but it does stop them from effectively using that one email address.

Malware Scams

Malware scams are a little different compared to the other scams because of the malware component. They might start as a phone call, an email, or some random link that you click on the internet. You might have visited a website that deposited something on your computer by way of the website cookies. Regardless of how they start, malware scams all result with some program being secretly deposited on your computer with the intent of doing you harm at a later date.

According to Wikipedia, "malware is any software intentionally designed to cause disruption to a computer, server, client, or computer network, leak private information, gain unauthorized access to information or systems, deprive access to information, or which unknowingly interferes with the user's computer security and privacy." [1]

Malware is *not* a virus, which becomes a cancer growing through your systems and corrupting files, often beyond repair. But malware can be just as harmful, if not more so, because malware can be used to gain access to your accounts that are not located on your computer. Through malware, hackers are able to gain access to your bank accounts, your taxes, and any other part of your life that happens to be online. Through malware, hackers can steal your identity.

In the past, malware (and viruses) were transmitted by passing files from one computer to another via an email or from a portable disk. But today, malware more commonly finds your computer by way of websites.

Internet websites employ a technology known as *cookies*. As a reminder, cookies are little packets of information, sometimes a specialized script, that feedback information to the website from your computer.

Most of the time, the cookies are a must. If you disable them (which you can do via certain settings within your web browser), the website might not function properly. Sites like Facebook use cookies to remember the logged in user as you navigate from page to page. Google uses cookies to help you sync your bookmarks between multiple computers. And sites that you happen to purchase things from, like Amazon, will use cookies to help remember your last set of purchase commands. But herein lies the danger.

Let's say that you've gone to a website that has deposited a malware cookie that records your keystrokes. This means if you were to go to a secure site, say your bank, then your keystrokes would be recorded, giving the spy your username and password.

And this is how the malware scams work.

Extra Hints to Avoid Malware Scams

Verify the Caller ID

For those scams that start as a phone call, verify the identity of the person on the other end of the line.

The phone call-based scams work only because people are trusting by nature. And it's this trusting nature that these scams prey on.

Microsoft and Apple will *never* call an individual about issues that they may have detected on your computer. Both companies are too big to care about just one person who brings them maybe $200 per annum of business.

But let's say that you get a phone call from someone who isn't claiming to be from Microsoft, Apple, or some other company like that. Maybe they're from a company you trust. Or let's say that they're claiming to be from a government agency.

I mention that last one specifically, because I once got a phone call from a man who *was* from the government, calling about a specific security issue that I had been having. I had been forced to factory reset my phone, and I was locked out of my government-issued business accounts because of it. I couldn't get a 6-digit authentication code I needed to get into the account because I no longer had access to the authenticator app that was connected to my account—and there was no way to bypass this. I had to put in a help request to regain access to my accounts. But when I got that phone call, I bloody well made sure that I was talking to a legit person *before* I provided any personal information. It helped that the guy was able to talk directly about the issue that I had sent the help request on. "I understand that you recently had to reset your phone and are now unable to access your account."

Years ago, I also had a phone call from the sales/technical support team that handles my virus checker. I was having issues with the latest program update and the system kept crashing as a result, locking my computer. I had to disable it just so I could put in the help request. It was a long conversation, with multiple checks to ensure that I was talking to a legit person *before* I granted that technician remote access to my machine. He needed specific log files that were embedded in a part of the system that I didn't have access to, the part of my system that the virus checker program hogs for itself. Tech support needed remote access so they could use the retrieval tools on their system to get the information the developers needed to fix the issue. But when that conversation was finished, the tech support person talked me through the process of securing my system again, ensuring that the portal created had been closed.

In both cases, I didn't just open the door without ensuring that I was talking to a legit person. I didn't *trust* that they were who they said they were. They had to prove it to me. I got them to provide *me* with information that only a legitimate person would know if they had direct access to my accounts.

And I recorded their names and other details for my records. Any legitimate call will be from a person who is more than willing to give you their name. If you have any issues with a company, you should be able to call the complaints office and give that name, and the person you were talking to should have recorded everything in your account notes for future reference.

Use Antivirus and Malware Detection Programs

Yes, I have mentioned this one before—way back in the beginning of this book, when we were talking about our internet security practices. But there will be someone who didn't bother to listen to that advice back when they read those chapters, so we're going to mention it again.

It's not always easy to completely avoid malware, even if you are diligent. Even without having been prompted by a scam call or email, you could inadvertently visit a website that deposits a virus or malware cookie onto your device.

The best defense that you can employ is to use a reputable antivirus and malware detection program on your devices.

Most new laptops come with an antivirus program installed. And this tends to be the first program I uninstall, so I can install a different one—one I trust and already have a subscription to.

I don't use the "free" systems, because they often use a limited database of viruses and malware. And the free systems have been known to slow my computer down after a few database updates. Instead, I pay for a subscription license to a reputable system that also acts as a home network firewall.

I won't comment about any particular program available—good or bad. Instead, I recommend that you to look at the antivirus software reviews from the past year on sites like PC Magazine (pcmag.com), PC World (pcworld.com), Macworld (macworld.com), or any other reputable software review site. (Yep, it's those sites again.)

These sites (particular PC Magazine) often run performance reviews, so you can see which software program would be the best bang for your buck. Don't look at the reviews that are listed directly on the software's site; those reviews will be biased to showcase only the positive.

And once you have whatever antivirus and malware detection program installed . . . USE IT! Actually have the program actively running in the background, always checking your files for any suspicious behavior. And if you are using a firewall (which you should be doing if you are surfing the internet), use it too.

My system has caught a few suspicious cookies over the years that were trying to take control. And zap. Trouble, be gone!

But dare I say it, sometimes, even with the firewalls and the antivirus and malware scanners, those pesky buggers still get in. When that happens, unfortunately, there is really only way to deal with them: factory reset and change the passwords to *all* of your accounts. It's a pain in the ass, but sometimes (as a close friend found out the hard way in 2021), it just has to be done.

Use 2FA

I know that I'm beginning to sound like a broken record, but seriously folks, I beg you. For the sake of your personal internet security, USE 2FA!

Use it on every system that you can. And if your chosen system doesn't have the option available, put in a system request, and start the campaign that the system developers put it in.

THE SKILLED HACKER

The internet is our world now. Every facet of our lives is now connected to the internet. But never be afraid of using the internet for fear of what the skilled hacker can do.

If a hacker wants into your systems, and if they have the skills to accompany that desire, they'll get in. There will be nothing you can do to stop them.

They won't need to stoop to using login scams to get your username and passwords; they have other tricks up their sleeves. Even the 2FA won't stop them.

But in reality, a skilled hacker is unlikely to be interested in you. You're a small fry.

No, the most skilled hackers on the planet have been hired by governments to hack into the systems of other governments. And the hackers who join the list of the FBI's most wanted often become the most highly sought after security consultants. Sobering thought, isn't it?

Look, I know I'm being the doomsday predictor over here, but the best way to avoid the scammers is to use your wits. Don't just blindly trust, because that's exactly what they are preying on.

REFERENCES FOR THIS CHAPTER

[1] Wikipedia (accessed: November, 2023) *Malware.* https://en.wikipedia.org/wiki/Malware

41
CYBERBULLYING

HAVE YOU EVER BEEN in a situation where you have given your opinion on something based on your knowledge and expertise, only to be shot down by one ignorant fool? Have you ever had that experience on social media? And have you ever found that when you chose to ignore the ignorant fool on social media that they kept coming after you—attacking your character? And, to top off the whole experience, did you need a friend to step in and handle it, for fear that you would explode on public channels?

I would be surprised if I encountered anyone who uses social media on a regular basis who hasn't experienced a troll attack at least once. It seems like a rite of passage to the internet world. For the most part, we're able to ignore the trolls, because they're after some strange definition of self-gratification, enjoying taking everyone else down into their dark hole of hell. But what if the troll is actually a stranger who we have openly let into our lives, influencing us?

When our interactions start on social media, we have no idea who will become a trusted friend and who will become the troll. It's a leap of faith. However, the internet and our habits on social media have become so integrated into our daily routines that when one person turns to trollish behavior, it can taint our entire experience.

Bullying behavior, no matter its form, is designed to make the one being bullied feel bad about themselves and to question their actions—and not in a positive way. Psychologists have spent years trying to explain to the public what effect a bullying culture can have on people's mental health and physical wellbeing. Bullying has even been linked to those committing suicide. There is a reason why there are anti-bullying laws and regulations in place to protect our youth while at school.

However, it has long been recognized that bullying is not restricted to just the school playground, but has migrated into the online world. New laws (and new applications for old laws) have been put in place around the world to protect us.

In New Zealand, you have the Harmful Digital Communications Act 2015. In Australia, cyberbullying is a crime under the Criminal Code Act 1995. In the Philippines, cyberbullying falls under the Cybercrime Prevention Act of 2012. In Canada, the nature of the cyberbullying will determine which act someone will be charged under, and the list consists of at least fourteen different acts. In the United States, the laws are state dependent.

But even though we know that it's unacceptable behavior (prosecutable under that law in many cases), we tend to let it happen and don't do anything to stop it.

Had the interactions occurred face to face and not over the internet, we would have no reservations in calling out a person's bad behavior. Yet, because the internet is involved, we say nothing for fear that we look like the bad person, tarnishing our good names on public channels. We just let the troll's comments and actions eat us up on the inside, damaging something just as valuable (if not more valuable) as our online reputations: our sense of self-worth.

For the most part, the people I meet in person are lovely and sweet, even the ones who I know for certain have none of those lovely-and-sweet traits in their makeup. You can have those heated discussions, but you can also control the situation to a certain extent, where you can wind things back a bit to get your point across. Those who take things to the extreme, being rude on levels that are socially unacceptable, are often excommunicated from our circle of interactions, and we likely go out of our way to avoid each other.

Online, however, mob psychology rules, and the troll attacks that seem to be the rite of passage have hardened many of us to the point that we are now filled with cynicism and are snarky in response. A small portion of our ugly sides leak through, but most of us can control our ugly natures.

However, because there isn't a breathing face that cries and shows emotions attached to that profile, for some people, this seems to give them permission to let go of all social niceties.

I don't know what it is about the internet in particular that seems to give permission for the worst behavior to come out online. It's like the computer monitor creates this perceived layer of protection that allows the monsters to come out and play.

And boy, do they play.

I have suffered from my own share of cyberbullying, events that I happily talk about on my personal blog. But because of my own interactions, I also know that there are no easy answers to the cyberbullying problem.

PLEASE TAKE ACTION

If you are feeling threatened in any way by a cyberbully or troll behavior, I beg you to take action.

Take screen captures of the bullying communications, ensuring that you include the date and time of those communications. Report the offending accounts to the service providers. Block the offending accounts.

If the bullying is happening in discussion groups or forums, ensure that the administrators know. If the administrators don't take action to deal with the bullying behavior, then leave the group. Your mental health is not worth the value that you might be getting out of the group in other ways.

And if the simple measures don't work (blocking and reporting), then take those screen captures and your log of attacks to law enforcement. There may not be a lot that they can do due to international borders, but every incident that gets reported helps in the fight against cyberbullying.

Do whatever you need to do to protect your mental health.

What good are your internet interactions if they are just making you feel sick and bad about yourself? If you spiral too far down into a state of depression, it will have a significant negative impact on your ability to write your stories—making the entire venture into building an online platform pointless.

42

Don't Respond to Reviews

As tempting as it might be, *never* respond to reviews, good or bad. It rarely ends well.

It's incredibly tempting to thank people for good reviews, and it's beyond tempting to go in and defend yourself against the bad reviews. But a response of any kind to any review is just opening yourself to a world of hurt.

Bad behavior over reviews from authors (and other creative types) is not anything new. If you dig through the historical archives, you'll find stories of where someone chose to trash a venue over a bad review. Other creatives chose to commit suicide—a little extreme, but it has happened.

Some authors have encouraged their fans to attack someone because they didn't like the review they got. And they encouraged the bullying behavior from behind the scenes, thinking that if they stayed away from it in the online setting, they could continue to look like the innocent party in the situation. Shame they chose to tell an entire room full of writers about what they did. And yes, this really happened. I'm the recipient of such an attack, and I was sitting there in the room when the author (who shall remain nameless) gleefully regaled the tale. I can laugh about it now, but, boy, I was seeing red at the time.

But some authors will even go online and rant about getting four (4) out of five (5) stars. No joke. It really happened!

In June 2023, an author preparing for the upcoming release of her debut novel went onto TikTok to rant about getting a four-star review. When I saw the article, I scratched my head and was completely bamboozled by it. Why would anyone in their right mind choose to complain about a four-star review, especially when it was only the eighth review on their not-yet-published book? All other reviews were five stars. But apparently, according to the rant, that was the problem.

The perfect score of five stars (with seven reviews) was destroyed by the four-star rating. It didn't matter that the review actually called the book "a really great first novel!!!" Because of one *stupid* move (the TikTok video rant, bad-mouthing the four-star review), the #BookTok community retaliated. They review bombed the not-yet-published book with one-star ratings.

And the vanity press publisher dropped the debut author before the book was even released.

I'm not going to go into discussions about this author's decision to use a vanity press to publish their book. That one was entirely their choice, but so too was their decision to go onto social media and show a darker side of their personality.

There were a few painful lessons to learn from the incident. The most important lesson:

> ## Do not respond to reviews!

Responding to reviews, good or bad, is only opening yourself up to attack.

If you make a habit of responding to the "good" reviews, the moment you don't respond (if that is the expectation you have created), people will know that you're hurt by a review—and the trolls will attack, because they know your weakness.

Don't defend your book against the "bad" reviews, because again, the trolls will come after you. They know your weakness.

Don't go public about bad reviews on social media, your blogs, or newsletters. EVER! (Complain to your support network through private channels. They will help you see reason.)

And if you feel the uncontrollable urge to thank people for reviewing your book on Amazon or Goodreads, thank them as a collective, not singling out any one reviewer.

Share with the public your reviews that come in from independent reviewers. Feel free to share only the ones that make you feel happy. But don't respond!

So many review disasters could have been avoided if writers would just learn to not respond to reviews.

PART EIGHT
WRITING IN AN AI ERA

43

THE LEARNING ALGORITHMS HAVE CHANGED EVERYTHING

THE PUBLISHING INDUSTRY HAS been flipped upside down in recent years.

The pandemic shifted marketing models, giving a lot of power to online bookstores (perhaps too much power). [1] Mid-2023, social media drove a change of the traditional publication model, where *influencers* got a say on what books were accepted for publication. [2]

But the biggest change that has impacted the industry in so many ways was the introduction of ChatGPT in early 2022.

The industry was filled with excitement and . . . well . . . fear. For the first time, a freely accessible artificial intelligence (AI) program was on the market that was capable of generating creative works based on a series of prompts. [3] While the technology could significantly improve things for some people, writers everywhere became uncertain about the full impacts that the technology would have on the publishing industry.

Literary magazines like Clarkesworld became inundated with AI-generated stories, and they closed their submissions portal as a result. [4] Amazon had a sudden influx of *self-published* books on the platform [5], and some of those books were fraudulently using the names of well-known, well-respected authors to boost their quick-buck sales. [6]

Many professional ghostwriters and copywriters began to question their future, knowing that businesses no longer needed to hire their services when they can get an AI program to write their material for free.

As we moved into 2023, a few things came to light about ChatGPT's creation that had the entire publishing industry in an uproar. There was a question of the legalities surrounding the documents and artworks used in training the algorithm. The question of copyright infringement suddenly was on everyone's mind.

Multiple lawsuits were filed against OpenAI, the company behind ChatGPT, including a class action lawsuit filed by the Authors Guild on behalf of many big-named writers. [7]

Writers around the world were lobbying for their local governments to change the laws, prohibiting AI developers from scraping an artist's work (visual, audio, and literary) for use in training AI without consent. And for the first time in history, the Screen Actors Guild and the Writers Guild of America both went on strike over AI usage in Hollywood, bringing Hollywood to a standstill.

There is no doubt about it. AI is a game changer, and the entire industry has been affected in one way or another. And with multiple cases still waiting to be heard before the courts, there is no way to know for certain where this AI thing will eventually lead.

However, how we react as individuals to the AI situation is a personal choice.

I personally have chosen to steer as far away from the AI-creation and AI-generation tools as possible. I will continue to use AI-assisted tools, but those still require significant human involvement.

The rest of this section within this book dives deeper into the legal and ethical reasonings behind my personal decision.

REFERENCES FOR THIS CHAPTER

[1] Cliff Guren, Thad McIlroy, and Steven Sieck (2021) *COVID-19 and Book Publishing: Impacts and Insights for 2021.* Publishing Research Quarterly. 37:1–14. https://doi.org/10.1007/s12109-021-09791-z

[2] Sophia Stewart (July, 2023) *A New Startup Proposes Influencer-Driven Publishing.* Publishers Weekly. https://www.publishersweekly.com/pw/by-topic/industry-news/publisher-news/article/92795-a-new-startup-proposes-influencer-driven-publishing.html

[3] OpenAI (2022) *Introducing ChatGPT.* https://openai.com/blog/chatgpt

[4] Wired. (February, 2023) *Sci-Fi Publishers are Bracing for an AI Battle.* Wired Magazine. https://www.wired.com/story/sci-fi-story-submissions-generative-ai-problem

[5] Greg Bensinger (February, 2023) *ChatGPT launches boom in AI-written e-books on Amazon.* Reuters. https://www.reuters.com/technology/chatgpt-launches-boom-ai-written-e-books-amazon-2023-02-21

[6] Jane Friedman (August, 2023) *I Would Rather See My Books Get Pirated Than This (Or: Why Goodreads and Amazon Are Becoming Dumpster Fires)* https://janefriedman.com/i-would-rather-see-my-books-pirated

[7] Authors Guild v. OpenAI Inc. Case 1:23-cv-08292-SHS Document 1. Viewable via: https://regmedia.co.uk/2023/09/21/authors_guild_openai_complaint.pdf

44

THE AI COPYRIGHT NIGHTMARE

AI, IN GENERAL, IS a copyright and trademark nightmare. If you look through the news, you will encounter article after article of one questionable act after another, all crossing the boundaries of copyright, trademarks, and author branding.

From publishers insisting on including clauses that grant them the rights to use a writer's work to train AI, through to charlatans putting out AI-generated work under a well-known name, we are only just now seeing the tip of the legal iceberg. And it will likely take years before it gets sorted out. But here are just a few things to keep in mind when navigating the AI minefield.

AI CLAUSES IN CONTRACTS

I don't want to spend too much time on traditional publication contracts, because that is not the focus of this book. However, for the completeness of the topic, I need to mention it.

For those writers seeking traditional publication, make sure that you read every inch of your contracts and know exactly what is in there. Make sure you understand what every clause means.

You should be doing this anyway, because those contracts specify how your advance is paid out and under what conditions your rights revert to you. But there are new clauses appearing in traditional publication contracts that revolve around AI. Some publishers want to use your work to train an AI program, so they can create more books in your voice without your involvement.

The advice from writers' organizations from around the world is to have those clauses stricken from your contracts. Get clauses added that forbid publishers from using your work in such a fashion. This advice is coming from the Authors Guild in the USA, the Australian Association of Authors, PEN International in the UK, and countless others.

With the court cases still waiting to be heard regarding the copyright infringement of those works already used in the training process, there is no way to know for sure if legislation will be on the side of writers and other creatives. It is best to act selfishly in this instance and ensure that your work is protected by your contracts.

Make sure you know how your work will be used by the publishers.

However, a large portion of writers are likely to never see a traditional publication contract. So, I want to turn this discussion to whether we, as writers, should or shouldn't take advantage of this technology in the creation of our works.

Not Copyrightable Under US Law

I need to highlight something that may determine whether you even consider using AI tools.

> The way the current US copyright laws are written allows for only works created by humans to be copyrighted.

In March 2023, the US Copyright Office put out an advisory note on this topic.

"In the Office's view, it is well-established that copyright can protect only material that is the product of human creativity. Most fundamentally, the term "author," which is used in both the Constitution and the Copyright Act, excludes non-humans." [1]

The advisory note goes on to cite court cases where the question of the "human" element has already been brought before a judge. Time and time, the rulings come down as stating that a work is covered under copyright law only if the work can "own their origin to a human agent." (Works generated by animals are also not covered by copyright law.)

This means, if you intend to publish anything that is using any component generated by AI (or your cat), then your work will not be copyrightable—at least not in its entirety.

This stance from the US Copyright Office was reinforced by US District Court Judge Beryl A. Howell on August 18, 2023, when Howell ruled on the lawsuit between Stephen Thaler and the US Copyright Office. Thaler had tried repeatedly to obtain a copyright for a piece of artwork that was generated by an AI program he designed, and his application was repeatedly rejected.

"Copyright has never stretched so far, however, as to protect works generated by new forms of technology operating absent [of] any guiding human hand . . . Human authorship is the bedrock requirement of copyright." [2]

I don't know about you, but this simple copyrightable fact turns me away from the idea of using AI in the creation of anything, including my promo material and cover art. I want my work to be protected, and if there is the slightest chance that it won't be just because I used AI for a part of it, then I'm not going anywhere near it.

Even if laws were to change to grant copyrightable status to AI-generated work, who should that copyright be granted to? The one who came up with the prompt that the work was generated from? The developer who designed the particular algorithm that created the work? The artist/writer/songwriter whose work was used to train the algorithm?

Is Copyrightable Under New Zealand Law

Now to drive everyone completely bonkers with how much of a mess this all is.

It turns out that in my home country of New Zealand, AI-generated material *is* covered under copyright law ... even if that work was generated overseas.

Here's the situation. The New Zealand Copyright Act 1994 already provides for literary, dramatic, musical, or artistic work that is *computer generated*, granting the copyright to "the person by whom the arrangements necessary for the creation of the work are undertaken." [3] And the act also specifies that *computer-generated works* are works that are "generated by computer in circumstances such that there is no human author of the work."

The act specifies the term of copyright on computer-generated works as "50 years from the end of the calendar year in which the work is made." [3]

Now, here's where it gets really messy.

Remember that case between Stephen Thaler and the US Copyright Office? One might be wondering what a US court case has to do with New Zealand, but it turns out that under New Zealand copyright law, Thaler already has an enforceable copyright.

Going back to the act [3], under section 18(2)(a), a work qualifies for copyright in New Zealand even if that body of work was created by "a citizen or subject of a prescribed foreign country." And a *prescribed foreign country* is any country who is a signed partner to any one of the many international copyright agreements that New Zealand just happens to be part of, particularly the Berne Convention [4]. So, by extension, any body of work created by an American citizen is covered under copyright law in New Zealand.

And a New Zealand-based copyright is enforceable in the United States, because the Berne Convention requires that contracting parties give reciprocating rights to copyright owners whose work is created in one member country and used in another member country [4].

And the entire creative world just imploded.

(I wonder if someone should point out to Thaler that he has grounds for appeal to the August 2023 court decision under the Berne Convention.)

This entire situation is a copyright disaster. For the sake of my sanity, I'm staying as far away from it as possible.

REFERENCES FOR THIS CHAPTER

[1] US Copyright Office. (March, 2023) *Copyright Registration Guidance: Works Containing Material Generated by Artificial Intelligence.* https://www.federalregister.gov/documents/2023/03/16/2023-05321/copyright-registration-guidance-works-containing-material-generated-by-artificial-intelligence

[2] Stephen Thaler v. United States Copyright Office, Case1:22-cv-01564-BAH Document 24. Viewable via: https://www.scribd.com/document/665871482/Thaler-v-Perlmutter

[3] The New Zealand Copyright Act 1994. https://www.legislation.govt.nz/act/public/1994/0143/latest/DLM345634.html

[4] World Intellectual Property Organization. *Berne Convention for the Protection of Literary and Artistic Works.* https://www.wipo.int/treaties/en/ip/berne

45

AUTOMATED EDITING PROGRAMS

FOR THE MOMENT, I'M going to assume that you're just as skeptical as I am about using an AI program to generate anything to do with your writing. So, let's turn our attention to automated editing programs.

I'm talking about programs like Grammarly, ProWritingAid, Hemingway, and AutoCrit.

In reality, automated editing software has been around for decades, starting with those clunky spellchecker programs that Microsoft created back in the days when everything ran on MS-DOS. (And yes, I am that old. I remember quite clearly when the program floppies moved away from the 5.25-inch disks to the 3.5-inch variants encased in the hard plastic.)

Those early programs followed basic spelling rules, and if a word wasn't in the computerized dictionary, you had to add it. (I always had to add my last name to those things.)

Microsoft incorporated a grammar checker into their systems in the 1990s, but it wasn't until the mainstream introduction of Grammarly in 2009 that people everywhere started taking advantage of AI to assist in writing their documents.

I use ProWritingAid to assist me with the grammar and punctuation stuff. Let's face it, there are so many rules out there that I struggle to keep them all straight. Unless I want to spend all day, every day, looking up the rules, I need something automated to help me.

Even Grammarly and ProWritingAid use AI

Every program out there today (even the ones embedded in MS Office) is based on some form of neural network AI. Each time you run a document through whatever system you're using, it gets better at detecting issues and distinguishing those issues from stylistic choices. The more you use the system, the more it can predict how you will phrase something.

That's the entire purpose behind using neural networks in AI programming. The system learns and adapts . . . just like a human would.

No one within the industry is up in arms about AI-assisted editing, because it is now industry standard. Editors agree that some programs are better than others, but in all cases, a human is at the other end of the system approving or declining suggestions. And some suggestions should be declined no matter what.

Someone please explain to me why "I was pleasantly surprised" should be replaced by "I pleasantly surprised me was pleasantly". I know that there is something to be said about writing while drunk, but ProWritingAid had completely lost its mind that day.

But I think that's the point. The AI program makes a suggestion that a human gets final say over. There are some writers who will blindly accept all suggestions, which is a huge mistake, but even if you take the time to carefully scrutinize the suggestions, there is a marked improvement in the final writing.

Editing Software Can Never Replace a Human Editor

When building software programs to analyze the way we write, the developers employ a set of rules to start from. They will build on these rules, enhancing the algorithms to match a writer's unique writing style, learning as they go—and hence the use of AI in the algorithms. Sounds good in theory until you discover that even editors can't agree which set of rules to start from—and how rigidly to follow them.

To quote Benjamin Dreyer, copy chief at Random House, "The English language . . . is not so easily ruled and regulated. It developed without codification, sucking up new constructions and vocabulary every time some foreigner set foot on the British Isles—to say nothing of the mischief we Americans have wreaked on it these last few centuries—and continues to evolve anarchically. It has . . . no enforceable laws, much less someone to enforce the laws it doesn't have." [1]

That quote was from *Dreyer's English*, published in 2019. It's a funny book about grammar. The entire book points out how crazy the English language is and how we frequently flaunt the so-called rules. Sometimes, breaking the rules is the way to go.

The top editors in the world will happily point out that there aren't really any rules for the English language, rather a set of guidelines that have developed over time. And these guidelines are known as style guides. But even the various style guides can't agree on the basics, including the use of the Oxford comma (also known as the serial comma).

Far too many times, an editor is forced to follow their instincts and go with what looks and reads best.

Therein lies the problem for the automatic editing programs. How do you program instinct into AI?

The concept of AI uses neural networks and a lot of training. Examples are loaded into the system, lots of examples. The more examples they can load in, the better the detection algorithms become. But no matter how much training you provide a system, there will always be exceptions to the rules. And no matter how good those detection algorithms are, they will always make mistakes—because we humans also make mistakes.

But some of our so-called mistakes are not mistakes at all, but deliberate writing choices.

FICTION WRITING OFTEN BREAKS THE RULES

ProWritingAid and I are often at war over the usage of passive voice.

In a piece of my own writing, ProWritingAid flagged the phrase *her arms were tied* as passive. Yes, the program was correct in saying that this was passive voice, because there is no mention of who or what is tying her arms (whoever *her* is). But when you look at the sentence as a whole, the passive construction was what was needed.

The whole sentence: *She went to hug herself to stave off the chill, but her arms were tied down.*

As the writer, I needed to choose between having something that makes sense given the style of narrative being used, or something that is so-called active voice according to a program. If I was to take on board the suggested edit from ProWritingAid without critical review, that sentence in my crime thriller would have read: *She went to hug herself to stave off the chill, but it tied her arms down.*

The suggested rework gives a *horror* feel to the sentence, with no real understanding of what *it* is. But that's not what I was going for. So, I ignored the suggestion and carried on.

Here's another example where the automated programs would have gone wrong.

Some time ago, a passage from a client came across my desk that described a character suddenly caught up in a tsunami. The writer had used a run-on sentence, something that had in the order of 60+ words in it, with no breaks. The effect was so powerful, because as the reader, I felt like I was tumbling with no idea of which way to turn—unable to breathe.

Any of the automated programs would have highlighted the sentence and told the writer to break it up and rework it. But that sentence was perfect in the context of the story.

(I would love to show you that sentence, but I can't, because of client confidentiality.)

Programs like ProWritingAid, Grammarly, and Hemingway have their uses. They are great for picking up the things I've missed in my 100 read-throughs of the same passage: words that were the wrong word (a few letters jumbled up, an *f* when it should have been a *t*, or anything like that); punctuation that is not quite right; and phrases that have become repetitive without me knowing it. But the human eye is still needed to add that subjective element inherent in writing.

As the editor, I'm okay with recommending that writers continue to use automated editing programs . . . as long as there is still a human making the choices about using the suggested rewrites or not.

REFERENCES FOR THIS CHAPTER

[1] Benjamin Dreyer (2019) *Dreyer's English* (p. 6). Random House.

46

GETTING HEARD IN AN AI WORLD

DISCOVERABILITY HAS ALWAYS BEEN hard. With the saturation of books on the market, many new and gifted writers often go unseen. While recent times have seen a tidal wave of AI-generated books on the market, believe it or not, it hasn't changed the difficulty level associated with discoverability.

With the introduction of self-publishing nearly twenty years ago now, agents and publishers were no longer the gatekeepers. The market became flooded by books written by all those who always wanted to write a book. Some of those books were . . . well . . . saying that they should never have been published is putting it nicely. But there are other writers, like Joanna Penn, who proved that just because they chose to be indie-published doesn't mean that their books aren't as good as the ones that were being traditionally published. In fact, some indie-published authors produce superior books that blow all the traditionally published competitive titles out of the water.

In a February 2022 article on Wordsrated, it was estimated that 1.4 million self-published titles were published through the Amazon KDP platform [1], with an additional 0.4 million books released through the Amazon retailer site via other avenues. 1.8 million new books in just 2021 alone. And this was before the tsunami of books generated by ChatGPT.

Only a small fraction of the books out there would ever be a competition for my own writing, with most books being in completely different genres. But even if only 1% of those books were competing titles, that is still 180,000 books. I don't even know how to comprehend that many books.

The idea of marketing in today's market . . . I'm absolutely terrified. All I can see are the dollar bills flying out the door for very little return. I guess that's a problem for another day.

CHARLATANS PREYING ON YOUR GOOD NAME

In August 2023, Jane Friedman alerted the publishing world of another level of scum that the scammers were willing to stoop down to. She had discovered that some charlatan had generated multiple books—all of which appeared to be AI-generated—and had published them using her name. [2] The books had even been added to her Goodreads author page. She was able to get Goodreads to remove them from her author page, and finally managed to convince Amazon to take the books down—after her blog post about the issue attracted the publicity of several big-named news outlets.

Since then, Amazon has put in place strategies designed to combat this level of abuse, but many writers don't believe that those strategies will ultimately work. In truth, the new technology is ahead of law, and new legal regulations are required. That said, even with regulation and restrictions in place, this type of scamming will always happen. AI only made the speed at which this can happen that much faster. And it made it easier for the scammers to emulate a writer's voice.

The only recourse you have against such an attack is to be vigilant, and keep an eye on what is being attached to your name. You may not be able to convince Amazon (or the like) to take down those scam titles, but you can at least convince them to remove the links on your author pages. And you can ensure that your fans know that those dodgy titles aren't you.

WILL AI PUT ME OUT OF A JOB?

Will programs like ChatGPT put writers out of work? Will the programs put editors out of work? It is this question that seems to be plaguing the industry the most.

The more I think about it, the more I think the answer is no.

There have always been the scammers out to make a quick buck. Every time there has been a new new technology on the market, there have been those willing to take advantage of it for the sake of the almighty dollar. But right on their heels have been those wanting to use the technology to our benefit, putting together the rules needed to remain ethical in the way we approach the technology.

ChatGPT is no different. It has been only a short time since ChatGPT was made publicly available, but already, you are seeing societal and ethical influences come to the foreground, hindering certain misuse and abuse of the technology.

As much as we might not want to admit it, ChatGPT and other programs like it are here to stay. Going forward, it's just another technology that I will have to eventually decide if I will use or leave for others to use.

Sure, there is no doubt in my mind that eventually ChatGPT will be able to write better blog posts than I can, but I don't think it will ever be able to properly capture the elements of my writing that are uniquely me—the human parts.

GOOD WRITING HAS A HUMAN ELEMENT

There is a subjectivity that comes with writing that evolves with conversation and daily practice. We develop cadences in the way we speak, something that stems from the menagerie of influences during our language development.

Yes, it is highly possible that a computer program will eventually develop in a similar way, but it won't develop in an identical way. As such, while a computer program might eventually be able to emulate the things I write, it won't be able to produce something exactly how I would.

In addition, writing has an emotional component that is near impossible to replicate in a series of binary strings. It's an odd phenomenon, but if a writer is crying while writing a passage, that level of emotional depth shows through on the page, and the reader is crying while reading the edited passage. I can't explain why this happens . . . it just does.

Because a computer is unable to feel real emotion, it is highly unlikely that an AI-generated story will possess the same emotional impact.

As a writer, I have nothing to fear from ChatGPT or other programs like it. My stories will still be *my* stories. They will still possess everything that makes my writing unique to me—something that ChatGPT can't take away from me.

Sure, I'll need to work harder on the marketing side of things, but that was always going to be the case.

As the editor, there will always be a need for the human eye on writing—because of the human element involved with the subjectivity of writing. For some things, mathematics and formulas can be used, making them perfect for AI-assisted editing programs. But so much of what I do as a developmental editor is about gut instinct.

You can take the same passage (identical action and core beats), but when written in one way, it feels stilted. Write it another way, and it comes to life. And it's not something that you can put a formula to. If you were to take the same writing styles and apply them to another passage, the opposite style reads better.

This phenomenon is known within the industry as *voice*, and it's something that writers and editors struggle to define and quantify. If writers and editors can't easily define it, how the hell is a computer programmer going to be able to program it?

AI has definitely changed the publishing industry landscape, but in my little corner of that world, AI has zero impact on how I will continue to work. I still need to write my stories. I still need to market my services. And I'm still a damned good developmental editor and writing coach, if I do say so myself. These are all things that ChatGPT can't take away from me.

REFERENCES FOR THIS CHAPTER

[1] Dean Talbot (February, 2022) *Number of Books Published Per Year.* Wordsrated. https://wordsrated.com/number-of-books-published-per-year-2021

[2] Jane Friedman (August, 2023) *I Would Rather See My Books Get Pirated Than This (Or: Why Goodreads and Amazon Are Becoming Dumpster Fires).* https://janefriedman.com/i-would-rather-see-my-books-pirated

47
FINAL THOUGHTS

BUILDING A PLATFORM TAKES time. There are so many moving parts that need to work as a cohesive unit, linking a complicated multi-dimensional puzzle together. And because of the way the online world is constantly changing, an online platform is never static for long.

Don't try to do everything right from the word go. Your platform, however it manifests, will continually evolve. Don't try to force it into a box when it wants to fit into a star-shaped bowl.

As I've tried to convince you throughout this book, not every networking site or tool is going to be suited to everyone. You need to pick the ones that you feel comfortable with and start with those. When you feel like you want to expand, pick your next online adventure, but choose wisely. If that shutter-bug Instagram site doesn't suit your personality, then don't use it, even if everyone else is doing so.

Keep in mind that this is your reputation here. Make sure that it's built with quality material, not just quantity.

Be careful of the time sink that social media can become. Ensure that you focus on your writing and keeping your website up to date. But more importantly, don't forget about your offline activities too.

Remember that a writer's platform is everything that you do to connect with your readers—online and offline.

I know a large portion of this book possessed a skeptical, negative view of the internet world. But the internet can open up so many opportunities for you as a writer. Just be smart about your activities and don't trust blindly.

The internet is our world now. Every facet of our lives is connected to the internet in some way. It has become embedded into the fabric of our society.

Because of my nature, I'm not your typical internet user. I see the new technology and I instantly start to think of how that technology can be abused. (It does help with the thriller writing.) But because of my nature, I also openly share my knowledge and experiences with others. I don't want to see people making mistakes that could have been easily avoided if they had taken a few simple steps.

It's heartbreaking to me to know that my close family and friends have fallen prey to the various scammers, and all because they are trusting people. Some of them didn't want to tell me what had happened, but I'm glad they did. While I wasn't able to help them clean up the mess left in the wake of the scammers, I was able to take their stories and incorporate them into my general knowledge on this topic. And I've been able to warn others of the dangers, in the hopes that others can avoid those hidden traps.

In moving forward, move wisely, but not in fear.

Don't be afraid of the skilled hacker, because the skilled hacker is highly unlikely to care about anything you do. Instead, take the steps needed to protect yourself against the opportunists.

Don't use the same email address for everything you do.

Protect your usernames and passwords.

Use 2FA where possible.

Be consistent with your branding and be true to who you are.

Don't feed the trolls.

And own your platform, but don't let it own you.

An online platform and the publishing cycle are all about the long game. It's the connections you forge and foster along the way that will be your reward in this work.

Trust me when I say that you are not alone on this journey.

SUPPLEMENTARY MATERIALS AND OTHER WRITER RESOURCES

THERE WERE A LOT of concepts introduced in this book. To assist you through the process of protecting your online platform, and to remind you of some of the hidden traps, a series of exclusive handouts and checklists can be found at:

blackwolfeditorial.com/hidden-traps-book

New resources are periodically added. Join the *Hidden Traps* mailing list to be notified when new resources are available.

If you found this book useful, please consider leaving a review on Amazon, Goodreads, or any other review site. That said, the best way to show your support is to tell others about this book. Help spread the word.

Also check out the other resources for writers available through Black Wolf Editorial Services (blackwolfeditorial.com).

Sign up for the monthly newsletter to receive updates and editing tips straight into your inbox.

ACKNOWLEDGEMENTS

As WRITERS, WE WOULD go insane if we were forced to traverse this path alone. It's important that I recognize those who have given me the strength to push on when I wanted to give up.

Thank you to Emma Lowe. If it weren't for you, I wouldn't have felt the confidence in my knowledge to write this book in the first place. Thank you for standing by me for over a decade as I put this thing together.

Thank you to Kathy Swailes for giving me a kick up the backside every time I became a chicken and started to procrastinate on what needed to be done. And thank you for reminding me that I can't do it alone. Because of you, I now have a new mantra: Sometimes, it *is* better to pay someone else to do it for you.

Thank you to the Writing Pirates. You lot make me laugh.

Thank you to Ellice Gullet. You kept me on track and reminded me to that I'm human too! Sleep is a thing.

Thank you to my other writing buddies of Eastside Writers: Carron, Rata, and Vera. Your spirit kept me going.

However, the most important people in this venture have been my husband and my two children. You have put up with the emotional roller coaster and burnt dinner meals, but you've loved me and gave me the hugs I needed to stay my course. I love you.

ABOUT THE AUTHOR

KIWI JUDY L MOHR is a writer, developmental editor, writing coach, amateur photographer, and a science nerd with a keen interest in internet technologies and social media security. Her knowledge ranges from highly efficient ways to hide the bodies through to how to improve your SEO rankings for your websites. When she isn't writing, editing, or doing something within the local writing community, she can be found plotting her next foray into mischief and scouting for locations to hide the bodies. (Shh . . . Don't tell anyone.) Follow her crazy adventures on her blog (judylmohr.com).

For editorial advice or writing tidbits, check out the Black Wolf Editor's Blog (blackwolfeditorial.com/blog).

www.ingramcontent.com/pod-product-compliance
Lightning Source LLC
Chambersburg PA
CBHW031236050326
40690CB00007B/825